Best o...
in au y...
do - I nope
you enjoy
reading this

Dr Shar...
Jani

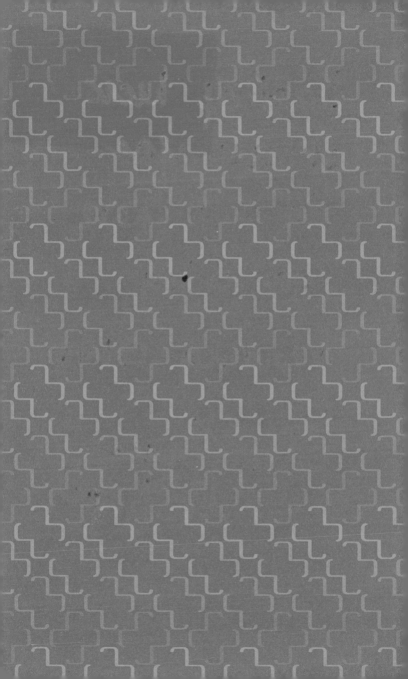

# ADVANCE PRAISE

Published by
LID Publishing Limited
The Record Hall, Studio 204,
16-16a Baldwins Gardens,
London EC1N 7RJ, UK

524 Broadway, 11th Floor, Suite 08-120,
New York, NY 10012, US

info@lidpublishing.com
www.lidpublishing.com

A member of:

**BPR**
Business Publishers Roundtable

www.businesspublishersroundtable.com

THE
POSITIVE
WELLBEING
SERIES

Printed in the Czech Republic by Finidr

ISBN: 978-1-911498-91-9

Cover and page design: Caroline Li & Matthew Renaudin

# POSITIVE
# MALE MIND

## OVERCOMING
## MENTAL HEALTH PROBLEMS

### DR SHAUN DAVIS
### & ANDREW KINDER

LONDON
MADRID
MEXICO CITY

NEW YORK
BARCELONA
MONTERREY

BOGOTA
BUENOS AIRES
SHANGHAI

Develop a better quality
of life, both physically
and mentally with...

**THE
POSITIVE
WELLBEING
SERIES**

**FOR OTHER TITLES IN THE SERIES:**

+ Resilience
+ Stress management
+ Health
+ Physical energy
+ Mental energy
+ Emotional energy

+ Nutrition
+ Fulfilling aspirations
+ Self awareness
+ Strengths training/
  wellness in the workplace

**thepositivewellbeingseries.com**

# CONTENTS

# ACKNOWLEDGMENTS

We would like to acknowledge Liz Guilford and the whole LID production team who have contributed to making this book a success. Shaun would like to dedicate the book to Greig for his unfailing support in all he does and to all the fantastic employees of Royal Mail Group. Andrew dedicates the book to Jane and his family for their great support over many years and to all his many male clients who have made their own journeys to an improved mental health.

# FOREWORD

As human beings we will all experience periods of good and poor mental health, just as we do physical health. Supporting mental health in the workplace is not just a corporate responsibility; employees who have positive mental health are more productive and businesses that promote a progressive approach to mental health can see a significant impact on business performance. So, it is about good business too – a real 'win-win'.

Organizations need to take steps to proactively incorporate better management of mental health into the everyday working environment, and it should be the marker of every responsible business to talk openly about mental health. Those that do not are less productive, less competitive and more prone to absence and employee turnover. Those that do attract the best talent and customers, and ensure they are successful for the long term.

My personal view is that all employers, and in fact leaders of every sort, have a responsibility to support the health and wellbeing of their staff as part of their health and safety duties, and at a national level. My aim is to help people lead healthy lives, both mentally and physically, and to achieve their potential.

Over the last few years, a number of landmark reports showing why and how employers must tackle the culture of silence on mental health have been published, and I have been proud to share my personal views on what can and should be done. The business and moral case is clear and I am thrilled that organizations are acting on the back of the published research.

I understand that acting on the evidence can feel tricky for some. This book will make that easier and help to ensure that everyone can work towards being a leader on good mental health, whatever stage of the journey they are at and regardless of their level in the organization. By reading here about what can be done, and learning from real life examples, you can act with confidence and make a very personal impact.

It is often said by organizations that 'our people are our most important asset' – this could not be truer than in the case of our people at Royal Mail Group. We are very proud of them, and the work they do, and I reiterate my commitment to keeping them as mentally healthy as possible.

We know that there are many ways to maintain positive mental health and, as you will see in this book, there are things that all organizations can do, whatever their size, sector or experience. This book gives some very simple tips and practical ways to help those experiencing mental health issues and ensure that they can stay at work, or return to work promptly and without stigma following treatment.

I wish you well, whether you are starting out or are some way into the journey, and I congratulate you on supporting such a worthy cause.

**Rico Back,**
Chief Executive Officer,
Royal Mail Group

# INTRODUCTION

As a society, we are arguably more in touch with our mental health than ever before and it is something we are becoming increasingly familiar with given recent media coverage. But, even so, it's easy to disregard its importance and the impact that it can have on our thoughts and our feelings, as well as the way we behave towards ourselves and other people.

Perhaps the term 'mental health' itself is a barrier, though it's really no different than physical health in that we all have mental health. We might get up in the morning and notice how we are feeling physically, but many of us rarely do a morning 'mind' health check, unless perhaps we have experienced mental ill health. Yet, taking our psychological wellbeing for granted is a cause for concern and we've known many colleagues who have been surprised when they shift in their working lives from a feeling of 'coping' to 'not coping'.

While many of the messages, recommendations and issues discussed in this book relate to both men and women in the workplace, we have written predominantly with men in mind. Women may have bought this book for men as a way to help support them. Our professional and personal experiences have highlighted that men, as a group, find it difficult to ask for support when they are struggling with their mental health. As men ourselves, we can identify with this. Men are a 'hard-to-help group', since they are often raised to be 'tough guys' and never show their emotions, as though that would be a sign of great weakness. This also poses a challenge for employers who are trying to reach out to and communicate positively with men about mental health issues.

Whether you are a man who wants to find out where to get support for your own mental health issues, a woman who's trying to help a man, a manager who observes a male employee struggling with their mental health or an employer who isn't quite sure where to draw the line when it comes to supporting mental health in their workplace, this book is for you.

**Dr Shaun Davis,**
Global Director of Safety, Health,
Wellbeing & Sustainability, Royal Mail Group

**Andrew Kinder,**
Professional Head of Mental Health Services,
Optima Health

# +PART 1
# UNDER-
# STANDING
# MENTAL
# HEALTH

# LET'S BE CLEAR ABOUT MENTAL HEALTH

Our mental health includes our emotional, psychological and social wellbeing. It affects how we think, feel and act towards ourselves and others, and influences how we respond and relate to other people and situations. Our mental health is also a key factor in the decisions and choices we make in our lives.

In short, it is the state that enables us to cope with the 'normal' stresses of everyday life.

Mental health problems can affect anyone regardless of age, gender, ethnicity or social group, and they are much more common than most people think. In fact, it is generally accepted that one in every four people in the UK will experience a mental health problem at some point in their lives.

These problems can range from feeling 'a bit down', and common disorders such as anxiety and depression, to less common but much more severe conditions that include bipolar disorder and schizophrenia.

Anyone can suffer a period of mental ill health. It can emerge very suddenly, develop as the result of a specific event or rear its head gradually and worsen over time. Some mental health conditions can be persistent and may be classed as a 'disability' while others might come and go, giving you 'good' days and 'bad' days. And, although some of us might be diagnosed with a mental health condition, with the right support we can still enjoy a healthy, productive and happy life.

Regardless of where you are on the mental health spectrum, it is important to remember that, if you have a problem, with the right support and treatment you can and will get better.

When we have positive mental health we can, as individuals, realize our full potential, cope with the stress and challenges that day-to-day life throws at us, work productively, and be a meaningful and contributing member of our communities.

Your mental health, just like your physical health, is impacted by a range of factors, environments and experiences. Some of these might be out of your control, whereas others can be influenced by you and those around you.

Some of the most common contributors to mental health issues are biological factors, such as a family history of mental health problems, and there is unfortunately very little you can do to change this. Other factors would include your education, self-awareness and life experiences, such as events in your childhood and school years, or incidents such as trauma or abuse. Such factors can be influenced and ameliorated.

Your workplace can also have a negative impact on your mental health. Unmanageable workloads or demands, poorly defined job roles and responsibilities, lack of control over work, an unhealthy work-life balance, poor relationships with your managers, colleagues or clients, organizational change or job insecurity, a lack of variety in work and a lack of career opportunities all potentially contribute to mental ill health.

Throughout your lifetime – and for some of us, even during the course of a day – it is perfectly normal for your mental health to fluctuate. Sometimes it will be good and other times you might need support, space or a little time to get things back on track. It is also possible that, while your mental health is generally good, you are also feeling stressed or anxious about something.

# MEN AND MENTAL HEALTH: YOU ARE NOT ALONE!

It is a well-known 'fact' – and something that we might even be guilty of joking about – that, compared with women, men are reluctant to admit they have a problem when it comes to their health. It's also a given that they are less likely to seek professional help for such a problem.

A recent survey conducted by Opinion Leader for Men's Mental Health Forum found that 46% of men with mental health concerns would be embarrassed or ashamed to take time off work. Some 52% of this group were concerned that their employer would think badly of them if they took time off due to a mental health concern.

And the chances of a man seeking help with a mental health issue seem even slimmer. Too often, men contact their doctor or mental health support services as a last resort, when things have reached 'crunch point' and have become too tough for them to cope with any longer.

A quick review of the data on men and mental health confirms that men have a tough time getting to grips with their mental health, and that this is a very real issue they face today.

- At any given time, 12.5% of men are diagnosed with a common mental condition, such as anxiety, depression, panic disorder or obsessive compulsive disorder. [C. Deverill and M. King (2009), 'Common mental disorders', in Adult Psychiatric Morbidity Survey]

- At least one in ten of the male workforce in the UK describes themselves as 'significantly stressed' and 34% of those surveyed agreed or strongly agreed they were 'constantly feeling stressed or under pressure'. [Men's Health Forum, 2016]

- Only 50% of men feel comfortable discussing mental health issues. [Business in the Community, Mental Health at Work Report 2017] Also, researchers found that 28% of men had not sought help for the last mental health problem they experienced, compared to just 19% of women. [Mental Health Foundation, 2016]

- Some 34% of men admitted they would be embarrassed or ashamed to take time off work for mental health concerns, compared to 13% who would be self-conscious about doing so for a physical injury. [Men's Health Forum, 2016]

> • More than three-quarters (76%) of suicides in the UK are by men [ONS], with suicide being the biggest cause of death for men under the age of 45. [Department of Health]

It is therefore no surprise that the odds really do appear to be stacked against men who find themselves struggling with their mental health.

But why is dealing with mental health issues such a dramatically different experience for men and women? Some argue that these differences are simply out of our hands and that the way men respond to mental health issues is just part of our genetic make-up.

While this debate will undoubtedly continue, this book is focused on factors we each have the potential to influence and impact, or that we can at least choose our response to:

• **Life experiences:** Childhood experiences, both positive and negative, have profound effects on our character, personality and emotions as we mature into adulthood. Because boys are encouraged to 'man up', act tough, stay in control and take what life throws at them – and actively discouraged from showing their softer side – as adults they may find it difficult to seek support when they're struggling with something, especially their mental health and wellbeing.

- **Social and cultural influences:** Compared with women, men are more likely to eat an unhealthy diet, be over-weight, drink excessive levels of alcohol, misuse drugs and be involved in an accident.

And where physical health is poor among men, it can have a corresponding impact on their mental health. Men also tend to have a very different social circle than women, with fewer close relationships, which means that if they're struggling with their mental health, they have fewer people to rely on or to encourage them to get support. Because men tend to focus on work relation-ships, they can feel particularly unsupported if a problem occurs at work – for instance, conflict with colleagues or their line manager.

- **The impact of the workplace:** There is a great deal of pressure on men. Even though society is changing (which is good news) the majority of men continue to earn more than women and are more likely to occupy senior posi-tions within an organization. Men are also twice as likely as women to work full-time and have a poor work-life balance, putting in inordinately long hours. They are also more likely to have the role as the main 'breadwin-ner' within a household.

Because work is so central to a man's life, when it is un-satisfying, disengaging or uncertain, it can be a signifi-cant source of mental distress and can impact the mental health of their family and those close to them.

Redundancy can also have an especially big impact on men, with their sense of purpose and contribution to their family and society more widely being questioned if they lose their job.

Regardless of how we got where we are, we do need to deal with the reality that men just aren't accessing help for mental health issues at an early stage. And that, of course, means that mental health problems are likely to last longer and go deeper. This will certainly change as the fantastic work being undertaken by government, employers, charities and mental health campaigners begins to cascade down to those who need help and awareness most urgently.

But, in the meantime, this book can help you to deal with the 'here and now' of your mental health experience and provide some advice, guidance and information on how to overcome any issues that you or those you care about might be facing today.

# MENTAL HEALTH, DIVERSITY AND INCLUSION

Although anybody can experience difficulties with their mental health, lesbian, gay, bisexual, non-binary, intersex and transgender people are significantly more likely to be affected than straight and non-trans people.

The Stonewall LGBT rights organization's *Gay and Bisexual Men's Health Survey* (2012) revealed some shocking data about gay and bisexual men and mental health:

- Almost double the number of gay and bisexual men were experiencing moderate to severe levels of mixed depression and anxiety than men in general.

- Bisexual men were more likely to experience moderate to severe levels of depression compared to straight men (26%).

- In the year preceding the survey, 3% more gay men attempted to take their own life than straight men.

- In the preceding year, half of gay and bisexual men said they felt that life was not worth living, compared with 17% of men in general.

The reasons for such high rates of mental distress among this community are varied, and are still being researched and understood, but some of the most common factors are thought to be:

- Stigma and discrimination combined with rejection and other negative reactions to being different.

- Bullying and harassment.

- Homophobia, biphobia or transphobia, leading some to not feel comfortable being honest about their sexuality or gender identity at work or at home.

- Negative reactions or hostility from family members, strangers and employers, which creates more tension and mental health distress.

Clearly this area of work is important for both employers and employees, and any programme to further understand these issues and provide support to those who are affected is going to be vital.

# ACKNOWLEDGING THE STIGMA OF MENTAL HEALTH PROBLEMS

Sadly, whether we like it or not, there is a stigma around mental health.

The stereotypes associated with men being expected to act tough – to be 'real men' without 'soft emotions' – contributes significantly to the stigma attached to mental health problems. These social conventions prevent men from reaching out for help when their mental health is suffering.

This stigma around mental health can create fear that you will be judged or discriminated against because of your condition. This can also discourage you from talking about your mental health and seeking support. As a result, it can feel impossible to talk with anyone about how you're feeling. Consequently, hiding your problem and hoping that it will go away really does seem like the easiest – or perhaps the only – option.

A poll conducted by the *Time to Change* campaign in 2015 revealed that the stigma and discrimination individuals with a mental health problem face can be worse than the illness itself. In the study, 60% of respondents said that these negative reactions were as, or more, damaging than the symptoms of their problem, while 35% said that stigma had made them give up on their ambitions, hopes and dreams for their life. The poll also found that nearly half of people questioned (49%) felt uncomfortable talking with their employer about their mental health.

Unfortunately, this stigma won't go away overnight. But, on the positive side, things are changing.

Celebrities, influencers and the younger members of the British Royal Family are proactively talking about and raising awareness of mental health issues. They're highlighting the importance of talking and seeking help, demonstrating that we are all in the same boat when it comes to the potential to be affected by mental health challenges.

Employers are also undertaking initiatives to promote positive mental health and educate their employees. Apart from simply being the right thing to do, it makes business sense for an organization to create a culture where employees feel able to talk openly about any topic – especially their mental and physical health – and seek support without being judged or discriminated against.

Looking at the UK, initiatives like the mental health charity Mind's *Time to Change* campaign are working hard to end the stigma and discrimination faced by those who experience mental health problems. Since the campaign began in 2007, Mind reports an improvement of 8.3% in public attitudes towards people with mental health problems.

Clearly, changes happening in the wider world don't always feel like they apply to you in your day-to-day life. Regardless of all the good work being done to eliminate the stigma associated with mental health problems, your reality might be very different.

But, take it from us, mental health problems can affect anyone, and there are people and organizations who can and will help you. You have nothing to be ashamed of.

We are all in the same boat when it comes to the potential to be affected by mental health challenges.

## SIGNS AND SYMPTOMS THAT YOU MIGHT BE STRUGGLING WITH YOUR MENTAL HEALTH

The specific signs and symptoms of mental health difficulties will vary depending on the individual affected and the nature and extent of their mental health condition.

That said, there are quite a few symptoms that could indicate a mental health problem:

- Mood swings
- Low mood, feeling numb or sad, or like nothing matters
- Personality change
- Self-harm or suicidal thinking or behaviours
- Reduced concentration, reasoning or decision-making ability
- Difficulty understanding or relating to circumstances or other people
- Detachment from reality; becoming delusional, paranoid or experiencing hallucinations
- Excessive anger, aggression or violent behaviour
- Eating too much or too little

- Increased intake of alcohol, tobacco, drugs or medication
- Withdrawal and isolation; pulling away from people and regular activities
- Lack of interest or motivation
- Tearfulness or feeling sad for no obvious reason
- Irritability
- Excessive tiredness; having little or no energy
- Feeling anxious, on edge, upset, worried or scared
- Being unable to perform daily tasks, such as looking after children or getting to work

Of course, these may indicate that you're going through some form of difficulty or physical illness, not necessarily a mental health problem. We should acknowledge that each mental health condition will have specific signs and symptoms, but looking at the broader indicators listed here and recognizing them in yourself or someone close to you is the starting point to getting some help.

If any of these symptoms sound familiar, it is probably time to talk to a trusted friend or co-worker, or someone at home. If you're becoming concerned, seek out a professional who can help you get on the road to recovery.

# STRESS, PRESSURE AND MENTAL HEALTH

Every day it seems that we hear a friend, colleague or person in the street declaring that they feel 'stressed'. And, although we use the term a lot, it can be hard to define exactly what it means.

It is probably not helpful to know that 'stress' is not in itself a medical term. There is no medical definition of 'stress' and there is, in fact, ongoing debate about whether stress is the cause of problems you're experiencing or the result of them.

The UK's health and safety regulator has helpfully defined stress as the "adverse reaction people have to excessive pressures or other types of demand placed on them". Essentially, it is a set of reactions and responses that we each have to the day-to-day pressures we experience. In the rest of this chapter we will refer to 'stress' as meaning excessive pressure.

There are a lot of useful resources and information relating to stress on this regulator's website – take a look at www.hse.gov.uk.

Whether stress is a mental health problem really depends on us as individuals.

We all react differently to pressure and, like it or not, it is a normal part of life that isn't going to go away. One person might find it a strong source of motivation and be energized by stress, whereas someone else might be overwhelmed by it and struggle to cope under pressure. An individual's response to it can also depend on what else is going on in their personal or work life.

Stress can cause mental health problems, leading to anxiety and depression, or making these and other mental health conditions worse. In turn, mental health problems can increase stress, as when struggling to cope with day-to-day symptoms and treatments.

If you think you might be suffering from stress, there are some physical and emotional symptoms that you might be able to identify. These include difficulty sleeping, tearfulness, exhaustion, headaches, neck or back pain, obsessive behaviour, heart palpitations, panic attacks, feelings of pointlessness or futility, struggling to focus or concentrate, or eating, smoking or drinking more than you normally would.

And, in the workplace, you might find yourself having more conflict with your associates, struggling with the pressures of work, finding reasons to take more time off or finding it difficult to get to work on time. You might also notice a decline in your performance and that you're delivering less work than usual.

# TAKING POSITIVE ACTION AGAINST STRESS

If you are feeling stressed, it is highly likely that you need to take notice – and take action – to change things. Fortunately, there are positive steps you can take to respond to and minimize this feeling in your life.

## 1. Keep on top of your physical and emotional health

Because your lifestyle is intrinsically linked to your mental and physical health, it follows that a healthy lifestyle will help you to stay alert and cope well, should things become stressful. This means paying attention to eating healthily, keeping fit, making time to relax, not smoking and watching how much alcohol you're drinking.

- Keep yourself moving because regular exercise will increase your capacity to cope with stress. It releases those 'feel good hormones', endorphins, and helps give you a sense of perspective and 'time out' if pressure does start to increase. Of course, if you haven't been keeping yourself moving recently, it is always best to visit your doctor for a check-up before you launch into an exercise programme.

- Most of us are familiar with the idea of eating at least five portions of fruit and vegetables, as well as drinking up to two litres of water, every day. It is equally important to eat foods rich in starches and fibre, choose fish or lean cuts of meat and poultry, and avoid too much salty or sugary food. All of this will help you manage your stress levels and maintain good physical health.

- Moderate alcohol consumption isn't necessarily a bad thing, but if you're feeling stressed there is a danger that you may come to rely on a drink to help manage your stress, rather than addressing the factors that are causing it. The same can be said of smoking. Cutting down or cutting out both of these temptations will have a positive effect on your physical and mental health.

## 2. Look at how organized you really are

A major factor in our increasing stress levels is feeling that we have a lack of control over our lives, whether that's our home and family life or our workload and what we're being asked to do or get involved in at work. But introducing a few simple rules for managing your day-to-day responsibilities can make a massive difference in how stressed we're feeling.

- **Use one method to organize your day and your life**: Whether it's a paper diary, an electronic one on your PC at work or an app on your phone, keeping everything well ordered, in one place, will reduce the chances of you double-booking yourself and missing appointments.

It will also help you to spot times when things will get busy and potentially stressful, giving you the chance to make alternative arrangements before it is too late.

- **Take a break at every opportunity**: This works on a range of levels, but each one will help to minimize your feelings of stress as you try to get everything done:

  - Rather than booking back-to-back appointments, give yourself some breathing space between each one to gather your thoughts, sort any actions you have from your previous appointment or just grab a breather.

  - The same is true for lunch breaks, and unless you've mastered time travel, remember to block out sufficient travel time between appointments, whether they're across town or with a colleague on a different floor of your building.

  - Schedule some 'desk' or 'thinking' time that will help you get your admin work done or prepare an important piece of work. Make sure you block the time out in your diary so other people don't encroach on it.

  - Make note of all leisure or personal commitments in your work diary, giving them the same importance as other items in your schedule.

- **Be realistic about how long a task will take**: It is tempting to agree to ambitious schedules only to discover later that they are just impossible to deliver on. Try to give yourself too much time to get something done rather than creating your own sense of pressure to meet an unrealistic deadline.

- **Keep communicating, especially if things aren't going to plan**: If someone isn't following the 'rules' to book appointments or tasks in your diary, and that is putting you under pressure, make sure you let them know and explain how to better manage it all. Politely, of course!

If you are struggling to deliver a task or project on time, talk to your customer or the project team about it. Sharing the problem and finding a solution that works for everyone is the best way to reduce the stress that you're feeling.

### 3. Stop... and relax!

The thought of relaxing when you're feeling stressed might seem impossible, but developing your ability to unwind after you've had a bad day will reduce your stress levels and help give you a positive outlook moving forward.

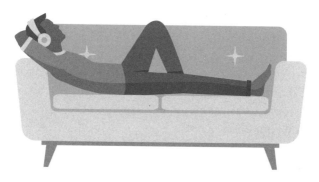

When you are stressed and become tense, upset or nervous, muscles in your body will naturally tighten. You might feel hot, sweaty or on edge, your heart may be racing and your breathing could seem faster and more shallow than usual. If you can find a relaxation technique that works for you when you're feeling like this, you can better manage the situations that are making you feel stressed.

- Learning how to control your breathing is an important part of being able to relax effectively. You can do this by following the simple instructions below, but don't forget to consult your doctor before undertaking a new exercise regimen or if this technique causes you any discomfort.

  - Lay on the floor, placing one hand on your abdomen (or stomach) and the other on your upper chest. Relax like this for a few minutes so you get used to your breathing. You can feel the rise and fall of the breathing with your hands.

  - Then, inhale slowly and deeply and try to push out your lower hand by using your stomach as you breathe in. As you continue to inhale and exhale deeply see if you can do this while keeping your rib cage and upper hand still – so your lower hand on your stomach is pushed up and down but the upper hand on your chest is not.

‣ Exhale through your mouth, making a quiet 'whoosh-ing' noise as you blow out gently.

‣ Continue to breathe in and out slowly.

Repeat this daily for about ten minutes for the greatest benefit, and with practice you should be able to slow your breathing down to about four or five breaths per minute.

Another exercise you can try, either sitting or lying down, is to breathe in through your nose, counting up to five, and then gradually letting your breath come out through your mouth, counting up to eight as you breathe out. Repeat this, trying to double the duration of your breaths out compared with your breaths in.

## 4. Change the way you think
A positive mental attitude will definitely help you to cope when you're feeling stressed or under pressure. We have all been guilty of thinking irrationally about a person or a situation, and that does nothing to solve the problem we believe we're experiencing.

• You think things are 'all or nothing' e.g.[1] if something falls slightly short of perfection or success you consider it a total failure.

• You see a single negative event or experience as a con-stant pattern of defeat and, even though it might have only happened once, you use words like 'always' or 'nev-er' to describe what has happened.

- You pick out one negative detail and dwell on it, obscuring everything else that may be positive about a situation.

- You jump to conclusions, interpreting things as negative even when there are no facts to back up your thinking.

The best way back from thinking in this negative way is to try and become aware that you are doing this – recognizing it is the first step. Try to use more positive vocabulary and take a step back from a situation to weigh up all the evidence before you reach any conclusions or make decisions.

### 5. Don't be afraid to put yourself first
Being aware of the importance of speaking up for yourself. Saying 'no' and putting yourself or your interests first can help you to avoid feeling that you have no control or choice over something.

Being assertive in this way means respecting yourself – this is who you are and this is what you do – and taking responsibility for how you feel, what you think and the actions you take. Here, it is important to let yourself make mistakes, recognizing that these will happen and that you can learn from them.

To help you put your interests and feelings first, you could adopt a number of tactics:

- Ask for time to think something over; don't be made to rush into a decision.

- Ask for what you need, rather than hoping that some-one else will already know this and take action on your behalf.

- Distinguish between having a responsibility towards other people and being responsible for them. These are two very different things.

It is easy to delay seeking help when you're feeling stressed, or to wait before taking positive action to change things yourself. Perhaps you hope that things will change natural-ly, or you don't want to ask for help because you think that would be an admission of failure.

Unfortunately, these matters generally won't resolve themselves.

If you're struggling to manage on your own, it is probably time to ask for professional help and guidance, whether that is from your doctor, your manager or from services such as your company's Employee Assistance Programme (EAP) or Occupational Health service. All of these are confidential and you are in control of what happens, but nothing can change until you recognize that you need help and are willing to accept it.

It is important to let yourself make mistakes, recognizing that these will happen and that you can learn from them.

# HOW BURNOUT FACTORS INTO THIS

When your stress becomes unmanageable and continues for a prolonged period, there is a danger that it can develop into what is commonly known as 'burnout'. This is not a clinical term, but an informal description of how mentally and emotionally run down and depleted you can end up feeling over time.

Burnout is a gradual process and it builds on many of the signs and symptoms of stress, creating a sense of mental, physical and emotional exhaustion that leaves you feeling helpless, disillusioned and struggling to gather the energy to do the simplest tasks.

When you reach burnout you really are at rock bottom: even the smallest problem feels impossible to tackle, you are constantly unhappy and the future looks bleak. Your energy levels will be low and the way you're feeling will be having a very negative impact on your family, your physical and mental health and your work. You've basically run out of resources to cope.

It is important to recognize that while burnout can be the result of constant and unrelenting stress in your life, it is not the same as stress. Stress can be the result of many factors, including too many demands, requirements or pressures in your work or home life. People who are under stress believe they will get better once they get on top of these things.

In contrast, burnout is about feeling empty and seriously lacking motivation. People suffering from burnout just can't see any hope or a way that their situation can change. They have no drive or energy to try and make things different, even if they wanted to.

Burnout can be caused by a number of different factors, and will be specific to you as an individual and the types of roles and responsibilities you have taken on in life.

- **At work** you might feel like you have little or no control over what you are being asked to do, you might be frustrated that you're getting no recognition or reward for what you're doing, and you might be anxious that you're not clear about what is expected of you or that too many demands are being placed on your time. It is also possible that you might be in a very repetitive, monotonous job or that your workplace is a particularly chaotic, high-pressure environment.

- **Your lifestyle** might contribute to burnout, with too much time spent at work so that you find it difficult to make enough time to relax. Or you might have taken on too many responsibilities with insufficient help or support from other people. You might also be missing close relationships or not getting enough sleep.

- **Your personality** might be such that you are just a perfectionist at heart and nothing you do or attempt to do is good enough. Alternatively, you might have a pessimistic view of the world and your place in it, or you are a 'high achiever' for whom nothing is ever quite good enough and you get frustrated by the slightest bump in the road. You might also just want to be in control and find it hard to delegate even the most straightforward tasks to other people, instead insisting on taking everything on yourself.

Some of the symptoms of burnout can be very subtle, but as they get worse the signs will intensify as your body absorbs the stress. That is why it is particularly important to 'listen' to your body and get some help before things get too bad. Taking action at the earliest opportunity will prevent a full-blown breakdown.

## HERE ARE SOME QUESTIONS TO CONSIDER:

Do you feel tired and physically
'drained' all of the time?

Are you suffering from frequent
headaches or muscular pain?

Have you spotted a change in your
appetite or sleeping habits?

Are you getting sick a lot, catching every
bug and cold that goes around?

Have you lost your motivation to do
even the simplest tasks?

Are you becoming increasingly cynical
and negative about things?

Are you feeling that every day is a bad day?

Are you skipping work, opting to call in sick
rather than tackle what needs to be done?

Have you begun to feel helpless,
trapped or alone?

Have you lost a sense of satisfaction with work, and life in general?

Does it take much longer to get things done, whether at home or work?

Do you find that you're pulling away and isolating yourself from friends and family?

Are you getting snappy and taking your frustrations and negative feelings out on others?

Have you turned to food, alcohol, cigarettes or drugs to help you cope with things?

Do you feel that nothing you do makes a difference or is appreciated by anyone else?

If you answer yes to some or all of these questions, there is a chance that you're on the road to burnout. Certainly, if you are feeling this way, it is time to give yourself a break and ask for some help. There is also a chance that you might be experiencing the symptoms of a clinical condition, such as anxiety, depression or both, so there really is no time like the present to seek help.

# TIPS FOR OVERCOMING BURNOUT

If you are dealing with burnout, reaching out to others is one of the most effective ways of dealing with how you're feeling. Just finding someone who can listen to you, who won't judge you or be easily distracted from what you're saying, is a great first step in relieving some of the pressure you are under.

If you are ready to deal with how you're feeling, here are some more tips to overcome burnout:

**1. Develop the positive relationships in your life**
- Invest time in those closest to you. Try your best to put how you are feeling to one side and just spend time together, focusing on the moment rather than what will happen next.

- Try to engage with the people you work with, just having a chat with them while you're making a cup of tea or arranging social events after work. This will help you to put work and what's being asked of you into perspective, and give you a sounding board when things get tough.

- Avoid people who are always being negative, especially if they are continually moaning and complaining about things. They will only bring you down with them, so it's best to steer clear!

- Team up with people who share similar interests with you, whether it's a sports club, a social club or a religious group. Meeting up like this gives you the chance to talk and interact with people who have the same interests as you, and it's a great way to get out of the house and expand your social circle.

## 2. Re-think and re-frame how you're feeling

- For most of us, it is just not possible or practical to quit a job we're not happy with and find a new one. So, instead, reflect on what you are doing and see if you can spot some value in it. Look at how your work might be helping others or focus on the small bits of the job that you do enjoy, even if it's simply the banter with co-workers during a tea break.

- If you are feeling frustrated and demotivated by your work, can you find a few hours to do some volunteer work every week? This has the potential to add some meaning and satisfaction to your life, hopefully without impacting your paid job too heavily.

### 3. Think about what and who you can change at work

- Who are your friends at work? Having friendships at work can reduce the feelings of monotony in your role, and laughing and joking with friends during the work day can reduce stress and keep you going when you're feeling down.

- But do consider whether the jokes and banter in the workplace are helpful. Are they actually a smokescreen that serves to avoid talking about the real issues that are occurring with not just you but also your associates at work?

- Can you take some time off? A great way to address burnout is to take a break away from work and remove yourself completely from what may be contributing to how you feel.

### 4. Re-evaluate and re-define your priorities

- The feeling of being burned out is a sign that something isn't quite right in your life, so take the hint and reflect on your goals and dreams. Have you drifted away from something that's truly important to you and makes you happy? What can you do to reconnect with that person, place or thing?

- Be prepared to say no, especially when people are putting unnecessary and unacceptable demands on your time. The first time is the hardest – after you've said 'no' once and freed yourself up, it will be much easier going forward.

- Set yourself free from your technology by making time every day to completely disconnect from your phone, your tablet, your PC and your Kindle. It is ok to be unavailable, so enjoy the freedom and accept the peace of feeling unconnected.

### 5. Exercise, rest and refuel

- Although it is probably the last thing you feel like doing when you're burned out, exercise is a powerful mood booster. Just 30 minutes' exercise every day – or even three lots of 30 minutes a week – can improve your mood.

- Make time to relax during the day, even for a few minutes. Sit quietly, close your eyes and focus on your breathing. Getting a good, quality night's sleep will also help to keep you focused and combat the symptoms of burnout.

- Your diet has a massive impact on how you're feeling and the energy levels you're able to tap into. Try to minimize your intake of sugary foods, as well as those with high levels of refined carbohydrates, trans-fats and preservatives. Cutting down on caffeine and drinking alcohol in moderation will also help reduce your feelings of anxiety.

Overcoming burnout isn't an easy thing to do, but it's not impossible. By taking the first step of just talking with someone else about how you're feeling, you can start to regain control of your feelings and your outlook until you're firmly on the road to recovery.

# TRAUMA

Trauma is defined by the Oxford English Dictionary as 'a powerful shock that may have long lasting effects' and it can relate to a wide range of situations and circumstances that present a real or perceived threat or danger to us as individuals.

Between 7 and 14% of people will experience a traumatic event at some point in their lives. [Rick J, O'Regan S, Kinder A, Early Intervention following trauma – a controlled longitudinal study at Royal Mail Group, Institute of Employment Studies, Report 435, November 2006.] Furthermore, about 10% of these will develop trauma-related illnesses and are likely to have longer-term symptoms that would benefit from professional help and intervention.

Traumatic events might include an accident, natural disaster, fire, car crash, violent attack, an act or threat of terrorism, or some other crime-related violence or threat.

How we respond to these events depends on a number of factors, including our previous exposure to trauma, how it was managed and the support networks available to us. Our personality, emotional resilience and life experiences, as well as our level of self-awareness and ability to express our feelings, will dictate how we react and recover.

In the immediate aftermath of a traumatic event we are likely to be in shock and distressed. Our heart will probably beat faster, we may feel sick and our mouth will be dry. Talking coherently might be difficult and our thoughts will be jumbled. While the way we feel will be disturbing, it is a natural reaction to our 'fight or flight' instinct and not a sign of mental illness.

In the longer term, our physical and emotional responses to trauma can be more wide-ranging and could include:

- Intrusive or unwelcome thoughts
- Difficulty concentrating
- Confusion and disorientation
- Amnesia or memory loss
- Nervousness and anxiety
- Withdrawal from people and situations
- Sadness, depression and feelings of vulnerability
- Difficulty relating to other people
- Anger and irritability
- Poor sleep and nightmares
- Increased or loss of appetite
- Increased alcohol or drug intake
- Hyper-vigilance and alertness
- Replaying events in your mind and obsessing over how you might have acted differently

Of course, most people who experience a traumatic event will gradually recover during the first few weeks following the incident. And while this recovery is unlikely to involve completely forgetting about what has happened, over time your troubling memories and anxiety will fade.

However, if these symptoms continue for some time, they're likely to start affecting your mental health. It is at this stage that professional help would definitely be beneficial.

Your mental health will also benefit from calm and supportive friends and family who are able to help you process what has happened and help you get back to 'normal' life.

# TIPS FOR OVERCOMING TRAUMA

Sometimes people who have experienced a traumatic event do go on to develop Post-Traumatic Stress Disorder (PTSD). If you are suffering from this condition, you will certainly require professional help to recover.

Fortunately, there are positive actions you can take to support your mental health in the aftermath of a traumatic event:

- **Accept that things take time:** It is important to acknowledge that it will take time to recover from your experience, but if you're still dealing with the effects of the incident after one month, you really should seek medical help.

- **Keep people close to you:** In the wake of a traumatic incident, it's tempting to keep to yourself and withdraw from social situations, but it is important to stay connected and keep people – especially those that you can open up to – close to you.

- **Maintain your routines:** Keeping to a regular routine will help to get you back on track. This includes sleep times, meal times and trying to get back to work.

- **Try and stay at work:** Work gives you the opportunity to stay connected with other people, in this case your colleagues. And if the trauma happened at work, you should access the support services within your organization to help you recover.

- **Stay on the straight and narrow:** Although it can be tempting to drink excessive alcohol or turn to recreational drugs to help numb the memories and aftermath of a traumatic incident, these can actually intensify your symptoms and 'self medicating' with them should be avoided.

- **Recognize that how you are feeling is perfectly normal:** Regardless of how you are feeling in the aftermath of a trauma – whether your feelings and emotions are more intense and unpredictable than usual, or if you don't feel anything different than you usually would – this is perfectly normal. We all react differently and we all need different types of support, information and reassurance to help us overcome the trauma we've experienced.

- **Take time to relax and refresh:** Keeping up with hobbies and pastimes will assist your recovery, as will making sure that you find the time to relax and unwind. This will allow your mind and your body to recover from the experience they've been through.

Ultimately, it is important to remember that trauma can be a life changing experience, and while it can be meaningful and significant at the time, most people do recover and it is important to be patient with yourself.

# MANAGING FEELINGS OF ANXIETY

It is perfectly natural to feel anxious, apprehensive or worried from time to time. Feeling like this is a normal reaction to a temporarily stressful situation like starting a new job, delivering a presentation, taking a test or meeting someone new, especially if it is an important meeting.

Most of the time, our feelings of concern subside as soon as the situation is over and we become more relaxed.

However, there are times when this isn't the case and feelings of anxiety stay with us for a long period of time, causing us to feel overwhelmed and panicked. As a result, our mental health will suffer, and over time feelings like this can affect our interaction with other people, our performance and attendance at work, our sleep patterns and our day-to-day routines. There is also a danger that the effects of anxiety can become overwhelming, and because we can't control these feelings we could become depressed.

The symptoms of anxiety will vary from person to person and at a psychological level might include fear, being on edge, irritability, difficulty concentrating and relaxing, feeling weepy and dependent, and seeking reassurance from others.

Physically, the muscular tension of feeling this way can cause headaches and your blood pressure will increase. Added to this, more rapid breathing can make you feel light-headed or cause pins and needles, and you might even feel nauseous. Longer term, anxiety can weaken your immune system and make you more susceptible to infections, and higher blood pressure can increase your risk of stroke, heart and kidney problems, as well as depression.

So, learning to recognize and control anxiety is an important step towards good mental and physical health and wellbeing. Fortunately there are a number of ways that you can help yourself.

- First things first: it is imperative that you **confront your anxiety and how it makes you feel.** Keep reminding yourself how much better you will feel when you've managed to reduce your feelings of apprehension to a more manageable level.

- You can proactively manage some of the symptoms of anxiety by using **breathing and relaxation techniques,** just like the ones you could use to tackle stress. Alternatively, listening to relaxing music, taking up disciplines such as yoga or meditation, or simply taking the time to enjoy a hot bath can help break the cycle.

- **Looking after yourself physically** is also important. Get some exercise and release some endorphins to improve your mood. But also try to avoid things like caffeine, cigarettes and alcohol, as they can intensify your feelings of anxiety. Trying to get good quality rest and sleep, and eating a good, balanced diet topped up with plenty of water will also improve your feelings.

- **Talking through what makes you feel anxious** will help to put your thoughts and feelings into context; it really does help to confide in a friend or family member, your doctor or a counsellor. Also remember that your employer may have invested in an EAP that can offer confidential support and information at any hour of the day or night.

# TIPS FOR OVERCOMING ANXIETY

Changing the way that you think is one of the most important things you can do to put a stop to your feelings of anxiety.

- When you start to get anxious, just stop what you're doing. Can you identify the feelings and patterns of thinking that made you feel this way? What is going on around you that could have contributed to you feeling like this?

- Can you see where your anxiety-related thoughts are originating? Perhaps you are looking at something out of perspective. Is there another way to look at or interpret the situation you're facing?

- Do you find that you assume the worst and just expect to fail? How do you think you would feel if you anticipated the best, or at least a somewhat better outcome?

- How do you regard the future? Can you look forward positively, or do you find yourself looking at the past and dwelling on things that have happened that simply can't be changed?

- Are you becoming overly self-critical? Feeling anxious can encourage you to be critical of yourself and others, so try to take a step back and look at the positives.

- Do you tend to blame yourself when things go wrong? How can you challenge yourself to re-think what has happened and why?

- Who else might have some responsibility for the outcome of a situation, and if you were giving advice to them, how might you help them to feel better about the outcome and themselves?

Trying some of the strategies here is a great place to start if you're experiencing anxiety and want to do something about it. But if these don't work for you, it is worth considering the professional medical support that is available via your doctor, EAP or a professional counsellor.

# RECOGNIZING THE SIGNS OF DEPRESSION

We all get sad or feel down at different points in our lives, and feeling this way is the body's natural reaction to a loss or change. But if these feelings are persistent or occur regularly in your life, there is a chance that they're highlighting the onset of depression.

The term depression covers a broad range of symptoms that can impact your physical and mental health and well-being. Milder depression – lots of us would just call it 'the blues' – can make normal, day-to-day tasks a real challenge. For instance, you might feel indifferent towards other people and what you are doing, struggle to concentrate and find it hard to make decisions.

When these feelings devolve into utter desperation or hopelessness, it is likely that the depression is severe or acute and there is a danger that thoughts of self-harm or suicide could accompany them.

Depression can affect people differently and at different times in their life. Some of the more common symptoms of depression include:

- Low self-esteem or self-worth
- Loss of sex drive
- Pessimistic view of life and the future
- Being unusually irritable
- Reduced energy levels and activity
- Feeling hopeless or helpless with strong negative thoughts
- Crying, or being unable to cry
- Self-harm or suicidal thoughts

Depression can be triggered by many things, from bereavement, bullying, loneliness and isolation to the loss of a job or a series of challenges and setbacks in life. It can also accompany physical illness and can be intensified by increased alcohol intake, recreational drugs, poor diet and little or no exercise.

Your doctor is a great first point of contact if you think you are suffering from depression. They can offer appropriate treatment, which could include anti-depressants and/or counselling. Your employer might also have set up an EAP or have an in-house counselling or Occupational Health service, which are great ways of getting some initial fast-track professional help.

# TIPS FOR OVERCOMING DEPRESSION

Alongside the professional help that is available for depression, there are also things you can do to help yourself:

- **Establish a routine:** A routine can help provide structure and framework to your life, especially if you're feeling so unwell that you are not at work. You might be surprised to know that being at work can really help with these feelings because it automatically gives you a structure and routine and can help distract you from the negative things in your life.

- **Keep moving and keep eating:** Staying fit and healthy and getting regular exercise will release endorphins to boost your positive mood, and when combined with a well-balanced diet you can prevent yourself from feeling sluggish and lethargic.

- **Watch what you're drinking:** Alcohol is a depressant, which means it slows down the functions of the central nervous system and can further lower your mood, especially the morning after! While it might be tempting to 'drown your sorrows', the benefits of this are short lived and could lead to even greater feelings of depression.

- **Seek out a self-help group:** Groups like this work on the premise that meeting, talking and interacting with people who are experiencing feelings similar to yours can help break down your sense of isolation and introduce you to new coping methods and strategies. It is also reassuring, and probably surprising, to realize that many other people, including well-known personalities and celebrities, struggle with depression. We're seeing more and more of them going on record to declare this as a way of encouraging others to talk.

+

# BEREAVEMENT AND MENTAL HEALTH

Reactions to loss and bereavement can vary greatly; there really is no right or wrong way to respond to this troubling and often unexpected situation. The way you feel following the death of a loved one, friend or family member, whatever your reaction might be, is perfectly normal and doesn't mean that there's anything wrong with you.

Some of the more common feelings you might experience include anger, denial and disbelief, fear, depression, guilt, numbness, mood swings, sadness, shock, lack of confidence and reliving memories. You may even experience a sense of guilt that you never expressed how you really felt about the person, or that there was a misunderstanding that was never cleared up before they passed away.

It is important to give yourself permission to feel the way you do rather than the way you think you should feel. Nonetheless, there are things you can do to help yourself overcome the emotional pain you're experiencing.

- **Give yourself time to grieve:** It can take a long time, probably longer than you initially think, to adjust to a major bereavement.

- **It can help to talk:** Talking things through, sharing memories and expressing how you feel can help you process your emotional reaction to the loss you have suffered.

- **It's also ok not to talk:** If you don't feel like talking, that is perfectly ok as well, but make sure that you do talk to someone at some point to avoid becoming too isolated and withdrawn.

- **Take things slowly:** When you are recently bereaved, you will naturally be anxious and worried and you might be struggling to concentrate. Be aware of the stress that you are under and take things slowly to avoid having an unnecessary accident or increasing your stress levels.

- **Don't feel guilty about moving on:** There will be a time when it is right to start rebuilding your life, so don't feel guilty when that happens. You're not being disloyal to the one who passed away.

- **Prepare yourself for the future:** There will be birthdays, anniversaries and other significant days that you will want to mark, especially during the first year after a bereavement. Think about how you can celebrate and commemorate these days, perhaps taking time off work or planning a special event with friends and family.

- **Gather keepsakes and memories around you:** Use photographs and other treasured possessions to keep your memories of your loved one alive. At some point you may be more able to celebrate their life, rather than dwelling on a visual memory of how they were when they passed away. Photos or videos of good times with them can help in this process.

- **Eat well, drink less and keep moving:** It is tempting to rely on alcohol or other drugs to try and numb the pain of bereavement, but in the longer term they can create other health problems, so it's best to avoid them or moderate your intake. Eating a balanced diet, getting some light exercise and taking plenty of rest will also help you to manage this difficult time.

In addition to the emotional pain of loss or bereavement, there are practical consequences associated with losing a loved one or friend, including housing and legal issues, childcare and support difficulties, as well as financial pressures. Arranging the funeral can create complications, especially if family members are dispersed or if there are tensions between people.

Talking with your doctor is a great starting point, especially if you find that your distress is overwhelming. They may be able to recommend a counsellor who can help you to adjust to what has happened and help minimize the impact of your bereavement on your mental health.

# SUICIDE

Suicide isn't something that we really talk about much as a society, which is a concern because it is the leading cause of death among men aged 45 and under [UK Department of Health]. In fact, more people die from suicide than from traffic accidents, according to the UK's Samaritans charity group. [https://www.samaritans.org/news/suicide-kills-three-times-more-people-road-traffic-accidents-we-urgently-need-act]

Suicide can be triggered by many different things, such as a long-term health condition or feelings of depression, hopelessness and despair associated with acute mental health problems. In the moment when you are suffering in this way, suicide might feel like the only option, but clearly there are other ways to regain control and achieve a positive outlook on life.

If you are having suicidal thoughts, it's important to talk with someone, maybe a close friend or a relative, or perhaps a health professional or your doctor. There are lots of organizations you can talk with anonymously and in confidence.

Additionally, if you think someone close to you is suicidal, it is really important to act on your concerns.

- If you think it is appropriate, **ask them if you can help.**

- **Listen to them**, without judgement or interruption.

- **Discuss your concerns or options in confidence** with someone who can help you, such as a professional who is an expert in mental health.

- If there is an immediate threat of suicide or serious self-harm, **take the person to their local hospital's Accident & Emergency department**. Alternatively, call for emergency medical help. Even if the individual says they didn't mean it, surely it is better to take the threat seriously and respond in an appropriate manner.

Many people can be affected by suicide, especially family, friends and co-workers who are close to someone who has taken this final step. Here, your emotional reaction to bereavement following a suicide can often be more intense, complicated and prolonged than if death was by natural causes. It will likely consist of a range of feelings, including:

- **Shock:** Finding it hard to accept what has happened or the way it happened.

- **Confusion:** Finding it difficult to reconcile or understand what led to such a final act.

- **Despair and sadness:** A sense of hopelessness and intense sadness over what has happened that has the potential to lead to depression.

- **Anger:** Directing anger towards the deceased, as inappropriate as this might feel, or their family or friends.

- **Blame:** Feeling that you or those close to the deceased may have missed clues about the person's intentions, and blaming yourself or others for not preventing the suicide.

- **Grief:** These feelings will depend on the individual, their relationship with the deceased and their previous experiences of bereavement, loss and suicide.

- **Guilt:** A persistent feeling that something might have been done to help the deceased, as well as reflecting on last conversations and interactions, and searching for clues about how they were feeling.

Each response to suicide is unique; some people may withdraw and find it hard to talk about what has happened, or prefer to deny what happened or how they're feeling. Other people may need to talk about their experiences. Whichever is best for those concerned, it is important that you do what feels right for you and, where possible, keep talking and ask for support and guidance as soon as you can.

# COPING WITH CHANGE

Change is inevitable, whether we make it happen ourselves or it arrives in our lives unexpectedly. It can be an opportunity or a challenge: our perception of it depends on us as individuals, and because change is a part of life it's something we need to learn to live and cope with.

Sometimes change can feel threatening, forcing us to face unknown situations. If we fear it, when it happens it is likely that change will worry or upset us and can negatively impact our mental health.

If we regard change as offering us a new and different set of options, it is likely that we will perceive it as exciting, allowing us to accept the change and believe that the choices it presents are within our control.

So by learning to accept and prepare for change, we can reduce the impact it has on us and our mental health. And, believe it or not, the ways to manage your response to change are relatively straightforward.

- **Think positively about the change you're facing**
  When it comes to change, most people have a great fear of the unknown and fear breeds worry and anxiety. It is too easy to be negative about change, but by trying to retain a positive outlook and focus on the elements that are within our control, we can respond in a way that will help to make it all a more positive experience.

- **Healthy body, healthy mind**
  We are more likely to have a positive outlook when it comes to change if we've been looking after our bodies by ensuring that we eat a balanced diet, do regular exercise, get quality rest and find a healthy work-life balance. This provides a strong foundation on which to prepare ourselves for the uncertainty of change.

- **Take a step back from change**
  When you're going through a process or a period of change, it can feel all-consuming. You can get a better sense of perspective about what is happening if you try and take some time out, disengage from what is going on and let yourself come back to things with a clean slate and fresh perspective.

- **Be prepared to talk things through**
  If you are feeling anxious or concerned about change and the impact it might have on you and your life, it is always best to try and talk things through with a friend, family member or a health professional.

- **Don't be afraid to get involved in change**
  Although it is tempting to avoid change, if you have the opportunity to get actively involved in it and express your opinion, it is more likely that you will feel comfortable with the changes that are being proposed. Having the chance to express your opinion and feelings about it will also tend to cast things in a different light.

- **Manage your expectations**
  Because change is unsettling, it is tempting to make assumptions and presumptions about what will happen and the impact of the proposed changes. Wherever possible try to ground your opinions in facts and figures and manage your expectations of what the likely outcome will be.

By learning to accept and prepare for change, we can reduce the impact it has on us and our mental health.

# LONELINESS AND MENTAL HEALTH

While loneliness is not in itself a mental health problem, the two are closely connected – having a mental health problem can increase your chance of feeling lonely, and feeling all alone can have a negative impact on your mental health.

We all have different social needs. Although most of us need some sort of social contact to maintain good mental health, some might be satisfied with a few close friends and others will desire a large group, with lots of acquaintances, to feel satisfied and content. In some ways this is influenced by our personality, so an extrovert will feel the impact of isolation more acutely than an introvert.

Of course, it is important to recognize that being alone is not the same as being lonely, and if you're comfortable with it there is nothing wrong with being on your own.

But if you are feeling lonely – perhaps because you don't see or talk to other people very often or if, even though you're surrounded by people, you don't feel understood or cared for – there are some things you can do to cope and feel better about where you are.

- **Think about how you can meet and connect with new people**
One way to overcome your feelings of loneliness is to try and meet new or different people. Perhaps you could take a class, join a local group or volunteer for a charity or community organization.

  Or, if you're not quite ready to meet new people face-to-face, you could interact with others online. Although online engagement may help alleviate loneliness, be careful, particularly if someone you didn't previously know asks for personal data and details like your home address or banking information. And, needless to say, exercise caution if someone starts pushing you to meet up with them in person.

- **Talk to people around you about how you're feeling**
Even if you do feel that you have a lot of people around you, you might not feel that they are giving you the care, attention, responsiveness and consideration that you need. The best way to manage this, as hard as it might seem, is to open up and explain to them how you feel,

perhaps suggesting how you think things could be different. There is every chance that the person in question didn't realize that their behaviour was impacting you in this way, and that they'll be willing to change.

- **Don't expect things to change overnight**
  Changing the way that you interact with people, or meeting new people, won't happen overnight. It does take time, so don't feel the need to rush into anything. If you are meeting new people, manage your expectations and don't expect full-blown interaction straight away. Take some time to acclimatize to a new group or situation and observe what is happening. Then, you'll be able to choose the best time to jump in!

- **Resist the temptation to compare yourself to others**
  If you are looking at social media, comparing yourself to other people and dwelling on how they're feeling, what they're doing and what they have achieved, you are going to be disappointed. A social media post only tells one side of a story – often projecting a carefully contrived, artificially upbeat online persona – so don't take any of it too seriously, and perhaps think about spending less time on your favourite social media channels.

It is also helpful to reflect on how your feelings of loneliness might be affecting your health. If they are making you feel upset, it will certainly impact your mental and physical health, so it's important to take action and make changes that will protect your overall wellbeing.

As mentioned earlier, the first and often most painful step is to recognize where you are when it comes to how to feel. This is the springboard to taking action to improve the situation and how you feel.

# BULLYING, HARASSMENT AND MENTAL HEALTH

Bullying and harassment – whether covert or more apparent – can happen at any point in your life, from school to work and every social interaction in between.

A bully misuses their power, position or knowledge to criticize, humiliate and destroy another person's competence, confidence, integrity and effectiveness. And when it comes to your mental health, bullying can have a massive impact, messing with your head and making you feel anxious, stressed and depressed.

Harassment, in distinct contrast to bullying, is any inappropriate or unwanted behaviour that could reasonably be perceived by the direct recipient (or any other person) as affecting their dignity, self-respect and self-esteem.

This could include suggestive remarks and gestures, comments, jokes or banter that focuses on age, creed, disability, nationality, race, sex, sexual orientation, family status, religion or any other personal characteristic. It can be a one-off event or a series of events that are carried out by an individual or a group of people.

Bullying and harassment can have a massive impact on your mental health and are likely to make you experience a range of challenging emotions and feelings:

- Anxious and worried, as well as sad and tearful
- Angry and stressed
- Worthless and unloved
- Helpless and hopeless
- Physically sick
- At risk of self-harm
- Struggling to concentrate
- Wanting to hide from social and work interactions
- Loss of appetite, or comfort eating
- Reliance on drugs or alcohol to cope
- Difficulty sleeping and relaxing
- Flashbacks and nightmares

**\!!/**

Bullying isn't acceptable at any level, or in any social or work situation. No one has the right to make you feel ashamed, frightened or lonely. If you are being bullied, you have the power to make it stop, and there are people and organizations that are ready, willing and able to help you.

- **Your doctor** is there to talk about what you are going through and how it is making you feel, especially if you are struggling with thoughts of self-harm, suicide, depression or anxiety as a result of the bullying or harassment. Make some notes before your appointment to help you mention all the symptoms that you are experiencing.

- If **your employer** has an EAP, they are on hand at any time to talk to you about what's been happening, in a safe, confidential and non-judgemental environment.

- **Other specialist organizations** may also be available to help you avoid future instances of bullying and harassment.

Beyond reaching out for professional help, there are also things you can do to take care of yourself:

- **Look after your physical wellbeing:** Eat well, drink lots of water, avoid alcohol and drugs and maintain a regular exercise programme.

- **Find time to relax and take a break:** Practice relaxation techniques and try some breathing exercises. They'll help you to relax, despite what is happening to you, and will put you in the best mindset to deal with the perpetrators.

Sadly, bullying and harassment do take place and people behave in ways that are, quite frankly, unacceptable. But remember, although it might not feel like it, you have the power to stop what is happening to you, so please take action if this is something that you're going through.

# MONEY AND MENTAL HEALTH

Money and mental health have a very close relationship. Worrying about money will affect your mental health and poor mental health can make managing money very challenging.

If this sounds like you, there are some positive things you can do to help yourself and minimize the impact that money issues are having on your mental health.

## 1. Think about how your mental health affects your money management

Consider how you spend money and why. For example, do you spend money to make yourself feel better when things are tough? Or have you had to take time off work, which has affected your income?

Conversely, is there an element of managing your money that affects your mental health? For example, are you anxious about opening letters from the bank or a credit card company? Or are you struggling with debt, but feel unable to pick up the phone to talk with someone about it?

Having a better understanding of your behaviour when it comes to money will help you to identify the best things to do to get back on track.

On a practical level, why not consider these tactics to help with money management?

- Avoid the temptation of spending and do something else instead, such as going for a walk or having a chat with a friend.

- De-register your credit and debit card details from online stores you may have bought from in the past, making it much harder to make a purchase when temptation strikes.

- Use online banking and web chat services if you find it hard to talk with your bank about money troubles. Most banks have a policy regarding customers who come forward with financial worries and they will be supportive.

- Recognize that you have an issue with money – many people do – and that by sorting out the money issue you will improve your mental health.

## 2. A problem shared... with someone you trust
Although it can be hard to start a conversation about money and your mental health, it can be hugely helpful to talk things through with someone you trust, whether it's a friend or a family member, your doctor or another health professional. This can be done in person, on the phone or online.

Also give some consideration to the impact that money problems can have on your relationships. It can be hard to talk to a partner about money or debt issues, and you might find it hard to open up to them if you need to rely on them for financial support while you are unwell.

### 3. Keep on top of the paperwork

Find a regular time to look at account statements, bills and tax notices so that you're on top of what is happening and there aren't any surprises waiting for you. It is also good practice to keep all your financial paperwork and other important documents together, so that if you do need to check something, you can go straight to what you need. Procrastination can be a problem here; it's tempting to put off working through tedious paperwork. A 'little and often' approach to tasks like this will help you avoid an unmanageable crunch down the road. However, if your paperwork is in a mess, it pays to start getting a handle on it today so that it will be better next time.

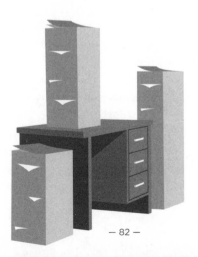

**4. Reach out to an expert**
If you are finding it hard to manage your money and it's affecting your day-to-day life and your mental health, seek advice from an expert. This could be an advisor at the bank, a debt management charity or your EAP helpline, which can direct you to someone who can help you work through the situation.

It is easy to underestimate just how much money worries can affect your mood, behaviour, performance at work and overall wellbeing. As such, it is important to acknowledge the impact of money worries on mental health.

# PART 2

# TAKING CONTROL AND TAKING ACTION

# THE IMPORTANCE OF SELF-AWARENESS

Self-awareness is an important characteristic that you need to nurture and develop in order to take control of your mental health and wellbeing.

It is the conscious knowledge of ourselves; this includes our character, beliefs, desires, qualities, motivations and feelings. Having a good sense and understanding of each of these aspects of ourselves can significantly benefit our feelings of engagement, success, satisfaction and contentment in our home and work lives.

Most of us have based our education and career decisions on things that we've seen or have picked up from those closest to us, including our friends and families. But as we mature and grow, these actions and choices may no longer suit our current character, desires and preferences. This is where self-awareness can help us identify alternative options that may be better suited to our individual preferences.

There are many tests that can help us identify and understand our character in more depth, including psychometric tests, coaching tools and self-reflection techniques. Having an enhanced understanding of ourselves has a wide-ranging positive impact on our working lives, such as:

- Understanding our own and other people's emotions more clearly.

- Improving our communication skills, encouraging us to interact with others in the workplace, including looking at 'blind spots' that are out of our immediate awareness.

- Enhancing our leadership skills, which can increase our performance at work.

- Increasing job satisfaction by concentrating on the roles, responsibilities and tasks that motivate us.

- Maximizing career development opportunities.

It is important to use our self-awareness to consider the impact of our behaviour on those around us and, when required, take positive action to adapt our behaviour. Self-awareness gives us the opportunity to think about how we interact with and influence others; it allows us to consider alternative ways of behaving and responding to different people and situations.

As part of this, it is useful to gather feedback from those around us, whether formally or informally, to learn about ourselves and the impact we and our behaviour have on others. Not being aware of our 'blind spots' can also be costly in terms of our career advancement because, in the work environment, a mistake may be remembered for a much longer time than successes.

Having an enhanced understanding of ourselves has a wide-ranging positive impact on our working lives.

# SELF-ESTEEM AND MENTAL HEALTH

Self-esteem reflects how much you value yourself and how important you think you are, as well as how you relate to other people. When you are struggling with mental health issues, it is highly likely that your self-esteem will be suffering too.

Although it is something that will build up over time and can be impacted by other people – including your partner, parents, siblings and relatives, friends, work associates and manager – there are things you can do to build self-esteem.

- **Understand the impact of change:** Your self-esteem can be impacted by the way that you react and respond to change. If you can develop a positive outlook on change, and be realistic about the influence you can have on an outcome, you can contribute to preserving and protecting your self-esteem.

- **Look after your physical and mental health:** If your physical and mental health is good, it will help you cope with the stress and pressure that life throws at you. Exercising regularly, eating well, drinking enough water and getting plenty of rest and sleep will ensure that you hold yourself and your wellbeing in high regard.

- **Make some time for fun:** If you engage in fun and pleasurable pastimes, activities and experiences, you will show yourself that you value your happiness, effectively increasing your sense of self-esteem.

- **Invest in your relationships:** Think about how much you expect of yourself when it comes to the relationships that are most important to you. What do you expect from other people, and what do you do to make sure that the time, emotion and energy you invest in your relationships has a positive influence on your self-esteem?

- **Treat yourself properly:** Do you celebrate your positive characteristics and achievements, or do you focus on the negatives? Try to avoid people and situations that will negatively impact your self-esteem and ultimately bring you down.

- **Take responsibility for your happiness:** Accept that you are in control of your own destiny and that you have the power to build self-esteem. Don't wait for other people to build you up or knock you down - take responsibility for yourself.

You can talk to a trusted friend or a professional about your self-esteem, and what you can do to ensure it's as strong and resilient as it can be, so that it contributes to positive mental health.

# RESILIENCE AND MENTAL HEALTH

Resilience is our innate capacity to turn adversity into possibility. Emotional resilience is our attitude and response to the people, places and things that we're faced with in our personal and working lives.

Essentially, resilience is our ability to deal with life as it is, not as you might want it to be. In fact, a common feature of people who lack resilience is not only the stress and anxiety they suffer when faced with obstacles and upheavals, but also the length of time and effort it takes them to get over that stress and anxiety.

What makes us less resilient as individuals can be factors relating to our upbringing, unresolved conflicts or simply that we were born with certain sensitivities to different kinds of stress and pressure. Regardless of the causes, there are a number of factors that can erode our emotional resilience and impact our mental health and wellbeing:

- **Highly stressful or traumatic events:** People who have been involved in traumatic events can find that they're less resilient to future shocks.

- **Experiencing several stressful events at the same time:** More than one significant life event or change at the same time will tend to make people feel vulnerable. For example, financial difficulties, threat of redundancy and the breakdown of a significant relationship happening together can have a hugely detrimental impact on a person's psychological wellbeing.

- **Experiencing stress over a long period of time:** When left unaddressed, cumulative stress can be as damaging as a one-off trauma. When someone is exposed to emotional pressure over and over again, their capacity to process it will eventually decline if the stress and its causes aren't dealt with.

- **Lack of control:** This can have a particularly damaging impact on the workplace. We are all given tasks we might not necessarily like or ask for, but those who have no choice over factors such as their pace of work or work patterns – or who aren't encouraged to use their skills or initiative at work – can be worn down quite quickly.

- **Lack of social support:** Social support is a key factor in boosting resilience, and individuals without friends or partners (especially men) are at a greater risk than those with an established social support network.

When faced with one or a combination of these factors, we can become deeply affected by stress. And should this happen, our performance at work, our decision-making and our mood and behaviour can all deteriorate.

# HOW TO BECOME MORE RESILIENT

If you want to become more resilient, it is important that you develop behaviours that will enable you to better manage pressure and promote your physical and mental wellbeing. Here are a few suggestions on how to become more resilient.

- **Build your inner toughness:** This includes the confidence to believe that you will survive and come through hard times, nurturing a sense of optimism and engagement with life and work.

- **Make sure you practice supportive thinking:** This is the ability to think in a reflective and rational way, noticing the effect of your thoughts on your own wellbeing, as well as listening to others and allowing and accommodating for differences in your personality and performance.

- **Find solutions:** Build your capacity to identify problems, set goals and apply solutions to maintain your mental and physical effectiveness in the face of possible difficulties or outcomes.

- **Create connections:** Be aware of your need for emotional support and think about how you can access this, making the most of feedback and support from a range of different people and sources, including co-workers and mentors.

- **Self-regulate your emotions:** Find a way to return to a calm state after feeling upset or emotional. Think about and analyse the potential consequences of your actions and your ability to switch off and refresh.

- **Implement positive life habits:** Commit to eating regularly and eating well, as well as relaxing and making time to refresh your mind and body.

Combined with these building blocks, there are some strategies that you can employ to deal with the triggers that impact your ability to cope:

- **Identify your vulnerabilities:** Before creating strategies that can boost your resilience, you need to know what you are up against. Try to become more emotionally aware, noting the times and situations when you feel stressed and overwhelmed so you understand your trigger points and can create strategies to address them.

- **Challenge negative thoughts:** It is easy to let pessimism become a habit. But fortunately, like any habit, this can be changed with a bit of effort and a lot of perseverance. As with identifying your vulnerabilities, you should make note of any negative thoughts you might have, challenging yourself when you recognize them and reflecting on how reasonable they are. Is there a way to re-frame how you're thinking and consider your thoughts in a more positive and logical way?

- **Accept what you can't change:** If you are resilient you will understand that a situation, good or bad, has to be accepted before it can be changed. Sitting in silence for a few minutes each day, breathing steadily and simply observing your thoughts and emotions is a great way to cultivate acceptance and boost your resilience.

- **Get some exercise:** Regular exercise works off stress hormones, promotes a sense of positive wellbeing and prepares you for your next challenge. If you find it hard to get a regular exercise programme going, start small with a regular walk during your lunch break. Even a little bit of exercise will make all the difference.

- **Make sure you have social support:** Studies on resilience often show that social support is vital to maintaining solid emotional resilience. If you have good friends or colleagues to talk to, reach out to them regularly. If you feel deeply cut off and isolated from those around you, it could be time to get a bit of outside help.

- **Create positive habits:** Whether it's exercising, spending time with friends and loved ones, or just making time for quiet reflection, it gets a lot easier to do something once it becomes a habit. Regularly setting aside short periods of time for resilience-boosting activities saves a lot of mental and physical energy and will make a dramatic difference to your life in the long term.

+

# UNDERSTANDING WHAT IS AFFECTING YOUR MENTAL HEALTH

You can't begin to improve, nurture and enhance your mental health and wellbeing until you've been able to identify the factors that are having an adverse effect on it.

The first positive thing you can do is to try and find the source of your stress. A great way to do this is to keep a daily record that details how you are feeling at certain points in the day, noting in particular anything that's making you feel stressed or unwell. For example, are there looming deadlines or regular meetings with clients or colleagues that are emerging as a trigger for you?

Ask yourself a few questions to help record how you're feeling:

- Where were you when you started to feel stressed?
- Was there a particular person or group of people involved?
- How did you react to the situation?
- How did it make you feel?
- How did you feel immediately after the situation?

By keeping a record of how you feel after certain situations, you will begin to identify patterns of behaviour that will give you the knowledge to take positive action to help yourself.

Alternatively, if you are struggling to identify the specific stressors that are affecting you, you might want to try a different approach.

For example, if you suspected that something at work was affecting your mental health, you could make note of everything you do and how much time you spend on each activity. Try and include everything in your job role, including responding to emails and the regular meetings you attend, as well as favours you do for co-workers.

When you review your notes, can you detect anything that might be causing you to feel stressed?

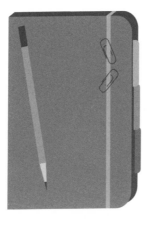

Some of the most common causes of stress at work include:

- **The demands of the modern workplace:** Busy workplaces mean it's easy to get overloaded with tasks and responsibilities that can, in turn, impact work-life balance, feelings of being in control, your home life and relationships.

- **Relationships in the workplace:** If you're struggling with people at work, including colleagues or managers, things can get difficult, and when relationships break down, stress levels can rise.

- **Uncertainty in the workplace:** You might have concerns about your performance at work or be worried that your manager is displeased with your performance. And if there are difficulties in the wider business and the market that you work in, you might be stressed about your long-term job prospects.

Now you have taken that first step to pinpoint the cause of your mental health issues, you are definitely in a much better position to do something positive about them.

By keeping a record of how you feel after certain situations, you will begin to identify patterns of behaviour that will give you the knowledge to take positive action to help yourself.

# SLEEP AND MENTAL HEALTH

Sleep is the biggest contributor to living better, so when things are tough, you're feeling stressed and your mental health is taking a bashing, it can be really difficult to get a good night's sleep.

When you're not sleeping properly and getting insufficient rest, you will feel weary, irritable and less able to tackle stressful situations. And when you start to feel like you can't cope, you enter into a negative cycle where you feel stressed about not sleeping and that inevitably leads to more sleepless nights.

The amount of sleep that we need varies for each individual but, on average, adults sleep for about seven and a half hours a night. If you do lose a few nights' sleep, it's not the end of the world. Although you might feel tired and grumpy, it will not always affect your overall mental health and performance levels.

Most of us are affected by insomnia at some point in our lives – in fact, one in three of us will suffer from this [https://wellbeing.bitc.org.uk/all-resources/toolkits/sleep-and-recovery-toolkit]. It happens most often when we're feeling stressed or under pressure. The underlying physiological cause is higher levels of adrenalin in our bodies, which makes it difficult to relax and interrupts our usual sleep patterns.

Of course, stress isn't the only reason you might not be sleeping. For example, are you taking any new medication? Have you drunk more caffeine than you usually do, or done so at a different time of day? Is your bedroom too hot or too cold? Are your neighbours being noisier than usual?

Our sleep patterns also change as we get older. We tend to become lighter sleepers and our sleep is more easily interrupted, so it's worth thinking whether this could apply to you.

The good news is that there are things you can do to help ensure a good night's sleep. Here are just a few of the options:

- **Establish a regular bed time** so you go to bed and get up and going at the same times every day, regardless of whether you feel tired or not.

- **Keep your bed for sleep**. Don't watch TV, eat or discuss issues that won't get resolved right before bedtime, opting instead to park any issues until the next morning.

- **Make an effort to relax before you go to bed** – maybe read a book, listen to music or take a bath.

- **Cut out intake of caffeine or alcohol** a few hours before bed and avoid having a heavy meal or spicy food at a late hour.

- If you haven't fallen asleep after half an hour, go to another room and **do something undemanding**, such as reading or ironing for 10 or 15 minutes, and then try again. But remember that even stretching out and relaxing in bed will give you some benefits, which is much better than tossing and turning for hours!

- **Redirect your thinking** by using distraction exercises to divert your brain's nervous energy. These can include remembering the names of football teams, counties or cities, the names of the people in your class at school, and so on. It's essentially the old idea of 'counting sheep'.

If nothing is working and you have regular sleepless nights, it's probably time to visit your doctor and ask for their advice. Along with insomnia there are other sleep problems – such as sleep apnoea or restless leg syndrome, as well as other underlying medical issues like dealing with pain management – that can impact your sleep pattern and need to get sorted out.

# TEN PRACTICAL TIPS TO HELP YOU MAINTAIN YOUR MENTAL HEALTH

Taking care of your mental health is just as important as taking care of your physical health. With the stress and demands that take a toll on our minds, we can feel anxious and under pressure, but with a few lifestyle and attitude changes, you can ensure that your mental health doesn't suffer.

These tips will help you to maintain your mental health on an ongoing basis.

- **Eat a well-balanced diet:** Make sure that you are eating lots of fresh, unprocessed food and drinking plenty of water. Taking care of yourself physically will pay dividends for your mental wellbeing in the long term.

- **Watch how much you're drinking:** Consuming too much alcohol, or other drugs, will put pressure on your physical health and after an initial high will leave you feeling irritable, tired and depressed.

- **Take some exercise:** Get moving at least three times a week to produce those 'feel good' endorphins and boost your physical health.

- **Find a way to relax:** Whether it's yoga or meditation, or making time every day for some breathing exercises, find a way to relax that suits you and your lifestyle so you can clear your mind and take a step back from what might be causing you stress.

- **Avoid negativity:** If you're constantly thinking negatively it will stop you from enjoying life. Work on learning to think more positively, perhaps seeking advice from a professional counsellor or your doctor.

- **Develop a positive outlook:** If you approach what's in front of you with a positive outlook, the way you tackle the challenges you face will dramatically change and you're more likely to see opportunities than problems.

- **Make time for yourself and your interests or hobbies:** Taking time out to engage in enjoyable pursuits can help you re-charge depleted energy and find the resources to cope with other areas of your life.

+

- **Manage your stress:** You're not likely to ever fully remove stress or anxiety from your life so the next best thing you can do is learn how to manage and reduce it. If you suspect that your stress levels are too high, it's probably the right time to get some help.

- **Live in the moment and go with the flow:** Try not to dwell on the past or worry about the future – it'll only increase your stress levels. Instead, focus on appreciating the present and where you are right now.

- **Sleep hygiene:** If you're not sleeping well this can negatively impact your decision-making, your mood and your ability to put things into perspective. Make a difference by analysing how you can improve your sleep hygiene, such as by not spending time looking at your phone when in bed.

Taking care
of your mental
health is just as
important as
taking care of
your physical
health.

# +PART 3
# YOUR MENTAL HEALTH AT WORK

# MENTAL HEALTH AND THE LAW

Even though your employer might be totally on board with promoting positive mental health in the workplace, it is reassuring to know that their efforts are backed up by law. This does depend on the geographic location, but there are legal requirements in the UK for employers to ensure that employees have a safe place to work, with support if issues occur. Most of these laws require that organizations protect psychological and physical health 'as far as reasonably practicable'. Health and Safety legislation highlights the importance of identifying and minimizing risks, and all organizations need to have a clear policy on this, including provisions for psychosocial risks.

More widely, mental health is all about valuing differences, and many national laws state that employers should not discriminate based on 'protected' characteristics such as age, disability, gender reassignment, marriage or civil partnership, pregnancy and maternity, race, religion or belief, gender and sexual orientation. If you are treated unfairly due to you having a protected characteristic or you are helping a friend or family friend who has a protected characteristic, this is likely to be unlawful (but do seek clarification of how your national law is structured).

# YOUR EMPLOYER AND YOUR MENTAL HEALTH

Work has the potential to have a positive impact on our health and wellbeing and organizations simply work better when we, the employees, are physically and mentally healthy.

Our mental health is integral to how we feel about our jobs, how we perform and how we interact with management, work associates and customers. Employers need to know that employees who have good mental health are more likely to perform well, have good attendance and be fully engaged in their work.

Because of this, it is important for an employer to take positive steps to improve mental health in the workplace, tackle the causes of work-related mental ill health, create a workplace culture where employees feel able to talk about their mental health, and support those who are experiencing mental ill health.

Forward-thinking employers will have a clearly defined policy to help ensure that a consistent approach is taken to mental health in the workplace, as well as highlighting the organization's dedication and commitment to promoting positive mental health.

In reality this will include:

- A statement of the organization's commitment to promote positive mental health for all employees and tackle the causes of work-related mental ill health. This should come from the top of an organization – the higher the better – and communicate the company's vision for creating a workplace where all employees feel able to talk openly about their mental health without fear of stigma or discrimination.

- A requirement for all managers and employees to receive mental health training.

- Recognition that an employee's performance or behaviour might be affected if they experience mental health issues. This will reassure employees that, if mental health issues are at the heart of an issue, appropriate support and accommodations will be explored before any formal measures – such as performance management and disciplinary procedures – are explored.

- A request for employees to seek help at the earliest opportunity, with the knowledge that their employer will do their best to support them.

- A process to reintegrate employees who have been absent from work due to mental health issues back into the workplace.

- Signposting for employees and managers, directing them to more information and support on questions, issues and organizations relating to mental health and wellbeing.

It may also be useful to reflect on how and what your employer is doing when it comes to supporting and nurturing your mental health.

- How do you think they are doing when it comes to identifying and tackling the causes of mental ill health in your workplace?

- What activities are they organizing to educate staff and management about mental health?

- Has training been offered to raise awareness of the signs and symptoms of mental ill health?

If you feel your employer needs to improve their support systems, you should take the opportunity to highlight what you think needs to be put in place. After all, the organization has a legal 'duty of care' towards you.

Employees who have good mental health are more likely to perform well, have good attendance and be fully engaged in their work.

## WHAT YOU CAN CHANGE IF THE WORKPLACE IS AT THE ROOT OF YOUR PROBLEM

If you're convinced that your workplace is adversely affecting your mental health, there are a few tactics you can employ to minimize its effect on you and your wellbeing:

- **Learn to say no:** Making sure you understand your capabilities, and recognize that time management is critical to avoid overwork. Only you will know when *possible* turns into *impossible* – one key skill to manage workplace stress is to say no when you should, and at the earliest opportunity. You may be tempted to take on more work than you can handle to win praise in the short term, but in the long term you might be asking for trouble.

- **Build a positive relationship with your boss:** A positive, two-way relationship with your supervisor can be a crucial factor in helping you manage your workload, and facilitating a conversation about resolving the issues that may be affecting your mental health.

- **Establish boundaries:** In the modern-day workplace we're reachable almost anytime, anywhere. And so, it's important to set boundaries, such as leaving work on time and not checking or responding to work emails after hours – at least not before bed or over the weekend.

Of course, you don't need to do all of this, and certainly not all at the same time! You just need to do what feels achievable and applicable to you right now. But small, positive steps will make a lasting difference.

There are also positive steps you can take to help ensure that your work environment is one that sustains and supports mental and physical health:

- **Be aware of negative or judgemental terminology and language:** Challenge this whenever you witness it, making sure to address gossip or negative behaviours immediately and directly. This will help create a workplace culture that does not tolerate harassment or discrimination.

- **Regularly and consistently encourage and promote healthy work-life practices:** Are there ways you can help promote an environment where everyone takes advantage of flexible hours, job sharing or working from home? Can you encourage healthy eating or physical activity among your co-workers? Are you going home at a reasonable time, taking the holidays that you've earned and taking any other time off that is owed to you? You shouldn't be expected to check work emails at home, so make it a habit not to do this.

- **Think about whether your workplace recognizes, appreciates and rewards achievement:** Do you and your colleagues feel good about what you do for a living? Are you confident in your ability to offer honest and objective feedback at work, taking the opportunity to learn from your mistakes when they do happen?

- **Encourage and support a work environment that promotes openness, understanding and respect for mental health issues:** Can you talk with your colleagues in a matter-of-fact way about mental health? And if they are struggling with this, do you treat them the same as you would if you were talking about any other workplace concern?

- **Help employees to help themselves:** Does your workplace have a policy around making reasonable accommodations when required? Does this happen in practice?

You shouldn't be expected to check work emails at home, so make it a habit not to do this.

# SPEAK UP AND GET SOME HELP FROM YOUR BOSS

It's a big deal to talk with anyone about your mental health, but particularly with your manager, especially if you're feeling anxious or distressed. It's tempting to just think that it is easier to keep struggling on, if that's how you're feeling at the time, rather than reaching out for help and letting someone in on what's going on with you.

In reality, there is no going back when you open up to another person and acknowledge your mental health issues. But if you are in a quandary about sharing your mental health struggles with management, it's worth bearing in mind that – as obvious as it sounds – the sooner you start to tackle your mental health concerns, the sooner you can make a positive change.

So, before you actually talk with your manager, take a moment to put yourself in his or her shoes: they are likely to be as nervous as you are about having this type of conversation. As a result, they might seem reluctant to talk with you or come across as 'cold' because they're nervous about saying the wrong thing.

This isn't your problem, it's theirs. Although you need to bear it in mind, their discomfort isn't something you have any control over and therefore shouldn't be something you worry about.

However, the more open and honest you can be with your manager, the better the outcome will be for you (as well as for your employer and team, of course). If you share all the background and information that you can with them, they can offer you better support, advice and information in return.

It's equally important to be aware that you have rights and should not be treated badly at work because of your mental health condition. Under the Equality Act (2010), employers in the UK have a legal duty to make 'reasonable adjustments' and not discriminate in recruiting, retaining or promoting staff (other countries have similar laws. Mental health conditions and problems are a disability under this legislation and employers should work in partnership with you to deliver on this duty.

There are some practical elements associated with talking to your manager about your mental health that you'll need to consider:

- **How do you want to broach the subject of a meeting?** Are you more comfortable emailing them or asking face-to-face for a meeting? Email is fine, but be careful about putting too much personal information in a note or using email as a way to 'let off steam'. It is hard to take back what you've said once you press send, and the contents of a note can easily be misunderstood and misinterpreted.

- **Be clear what you are asking for.** Request a one-to-one meeting with your manager and explain that you would like the opportunity to discuss some issues you've been grappling with, and how they relate to your work. Discuss the support your manager can offer you to help you manage your mental health and enable you to perform better.

- **Is there a location for the meeting that you would prefer?** Where will you be most comfortable discussing these matters? And would you prefer to meet with your manager alone, or would you like a trade union representative or a colleague to be present too?

Ahead of your meeting with management, think about how much information you want to share and how you want to frame it. Below are some questions and issues you might also want to consider, to put your mental health issues into context and prepare for some of the thoughts and reactions your manager might have.

- Is the cause of your mental health condition related to your personal or home life? What background and information on this are you prepared to share with your manager?

- Has there been a specific incident or situation at work that has exacerbated the problem? Or, have things been building up over time?

- How much information do you want to share with your co-workers? Do you want to request complete confidentiality? This is an opportunity to decide with your manager which colleagues, if any, should be informed and what they should be told.

- Opening up and acknowledging your mental health issues is an emotional experience. How will you manage these feelings during the meeting with your manager?

- Is there something that your manager could do to reduce stress or minimize the impact of your mental health condition?

- What support is there from the organization to help your mental health? This might be via your employer-funded EAP or Occupational Health team.

- What is your employer's sick pay policy? Can you self-certify your absence, if it's required, for a period of time or will you need to produce a note from your doctor?

- Is there a benefit to putting your doctor directly in touch with your employer? Or, will this make you more anxious about your situation?

- How is this meeting going to be followed up? Is there a way to track progress on the issues you've raised or monitor how you are feeling about things?

Once your employer is aware of your mental health issues, they have a legal obligation to support you, and your meeting with them is the first step in seeking help. What happens next will in large part be guided by your manager. Let them confirm what follow-up will take place, the timeline and what you can expect as the next steps.

But don't forget that their 'duty of care' does not replace your responsibility to look after yourself the best you can, and this includes actively helping yourself in whatever way you can.

## HOW TO TALK WITH A COLLEAGUE IF YOU'RE WORRIED ABOUT THEIR MENTAL HEALTH

We spend a lot of time with work colleagues, and as such we have an opportunity to play an important role if we suspect that they may be struggling with their mental health. But the sensitive nature of mental health means that it can be really hard for them to open up if they're struggling, so we need to be careful about how we approach the subject.

It might be immediately obvious that someone is struggling with their mental health, and you can take swift action to help them. Other times you might gradually begin to spot the signs and symptoms, perhaps over a period of weeks or months.

When the time seems right to approach a co-worker about your concern for them, it's important that the conversation be proactive, positive and supportive. Here are some tips to help ensure that it is:

- **Choose the right place to talk:** Where you decide to talk with a work associate about their mental health needs to be quiet and private, so the person feels comfortable and equal. You might conclude that a location outside the workplace is best, and if they work from home, you might want to meet with them there, on their territory.

- **Encourage people to talk with you:** People can find it difficult to talk about their mental health, but they are likely to feel less reluctant if workplace conversations about these matters are normalized, seen and heard on a regular basis.

- **Use simple, open and non-judgemental questions:** These will enable people to explain, in their own words, what they think the problem is and how it manifests itself. Can they tell you what the triggers are to their mental health issues, how it affects their work and home life, and what support they think would be useful to help them overcome these challenges?

- **Don't be tempted to make assumptions:** It's easy to try and guess what symptoms a colleague might have and how these are affecting their ability to do their job. But stop, and don't assume anything! Let them tell you how they think they can best manage their mental health and the support they would like from you when they're having a difficult time.

- **Listen to what you're told:** Everyone's experience with a mental health problem is different, so don't be tempted to think there's a 'one size fits all' solution. Have a flexible approach to offering help and advice, remembering that what might be right for you won't always be right for someone else.

- **Assure your co-worker of confidentiality:** People need to be reassured that you will treat what they tell you with confidence. Discuss precisely what information they want to be shared, and be sure that any subsequent third-party conversations are in line with the latest data protection legislation.

- **Encourage them to get professional advice and support:** Encourage your co-worker to talk with their doctor about the struggles they're having, as well as talking about other support services, such as your EAP or Occupational Health services, especially if you've had a positive experience using these services.

Throughout your conversation, reassure your colleague that your concern is sincere, and that you're ready, willing and able to talk with them. If the time for your conversation arrives and the person decides that the moment isn't right after all, assure them that you'll be ready to talk when they are and prepared to help whenever they need you.

Don't forget that your support can really help your co-worker, especially in an encourager and signpost role, rather than as their counsellor - leave this to the professionals!

# KEEPING IN TOUCH DURING SICKNESS ABSENCE

It is recommended that you do what you can to keep in touch with your employer and colleagues when you're absent from work, whether this is due to mental or physical ill health.

Not only does keeping in touch help address the practical issues, such as sharing information about your recuperation and expected return-to-work dates, but it helps keep you connected to your team. Your manager and your employer should provide you with the opportunity to address any concerns or worries that you might have as they arise.

Keeping in touch also helps to ensure that you're not isolated from your associates and friends at work because of your absence. Maintaining your connection with them and not cutting yourself off will make the transition back to work more comfortable for everyone when you're ready to return.

While you are absent from work, it's natural to feel nervous and it's likely that you will have lots of questions about the future, your job and what happens next.

Some things for you to think about include:

- Do you want to hear from work? Are you ok with management and colleagues sending cards, emailing or calling you to find out how things are going?

- If you do want people to keep in touch or visit, are there any questions or topics that you'd prefer to keep off-limits? What will you do if someone does visit or call and veers into areas you'd rather not discuss?

- Is it ok for you to pop in to work at an arranged time for a cup of tea, to keep you connected with your team and catch up on what's been going on?

- Is there a designated colleague who can keep in touch with you directly, let you know what is happening and relay your progress back to others at work?

- What support can your employer give you while you're absent from work? Is there counselling support, occupational health advice or healthcare services that can aid and assist in your recovery?

- Is there an opportunity to have a staggered return to work that would perhaps let you start off working a few hours a day from home?

- Are you worried about the security of your job? Or, is your absence causing any financial problems for you? What support and reassurance can your employer offer to allay these fears?

Make a note of any concerns and questions you have while you're away from the workplace, and raise them with management at the earliest opportunity so that any worries you have don't fester. Your employer and your co-workers will want you back at work quickly, but not until you're ready, and by keeping channels of communication open with them you can ensure that you keep your recovery on track.

# RETURNING TO WORK AFTER TIME OFF FOR MENTAL HEALTH ISSUES

Returning to work after taking time off for a mental health issue is a big step to take, just as it would be after taking time off to recuperate and recover from a physical condition.

When you start to think about getting ready to return to work, a good starting point is to consider the support or adjustments that would help make your return a successful, long-term one.

There are quite a few questions you might want to ponder ahead of your return to work, including:

- Is there a particular aspect of the job that makes you feel stressed or anxious?

- Can you think of anything that could be done to address this and make a positive change?

- Depending on the timing of your return, is there a project, event or deadline that you think you might need more support to deliver on?

- Would it be useful to lighten your workload and delegate some of your duties and responsibilities to a colleague?

- Is there an opportunity to work from home or adjust your working hours so, for example, you're not travelling into work during rush hour?

- Do you need any additional time off for more treatment or rehabilitation?

- What do you want your work associates to be told about the time you've been away?

- Are you ready for potentially uncomfortable or tactless questions about the time you've been away? How will you handle these?

- Is there any extra training that might give you a boost in your skills or confidence?

- How do you want your progress to be monitored when you're back at work? How often do you want to meet with your manager to catch up, and where would you be most comfortable having these meetings?

- What steps can you take to minimize the possibility of your mental health deteriorating and you needing to take time off again in the future?

- Is there an opportunity to informally meet with a colleague ahead of your return to work, to break the ice and get back into the swing of things?

In preparing to return to work it is important to reduce your expectations, as it can take a while to settle back in to to your 'normal' routine and you may initially feel more tired than normal. Do what you can to get ready for your return, and remember that there are lots of people and support channels available in the workplace if you need them.

# MAKING REASONABLE ADJUSTMENTS IN THE WORKPLACE

Making adjustments in the workplace is important to help you cope with mental health issues. These modifications can help reduce the length of time you're absent from work, and help keep you there – feeling good and performing well – once you do return.

The right adjustments will enable you to feel trusted, capable and empowered to do your job, and reassured that you're being supported by your employer.

Remember, you are the expert in how you're feeling, and as such you'll know best what changes, considerations and support you need. Communication is key to making the right changes, so have a conversation with your manager about what you can and can't do, so you can work together in partnership to find the most appropriate solutions.

While it might be tempting for your employer to micromanage you when you're struggling with your mental health, and make adjustments that reduce your workload, this isn't the right thing to do. In fact, adopting this approach could actually be counterproductive – if people feel that their work is not sufficiently challenging they can lose motivation and feel disengaged from their work and employer.

There is also a danger that if you feel your employer does not trust your ability to do your job, your sense of anxiety and mental distress might actually intensify.

When it comes to the type of workplace adjustments that can practically support you if you're struggling with your mental health, these don't have to be extravagant or complicated. Often the most effective changes are small and simple. Here are some that you might consider when discussing suitable changes with your employer:

- Can flexible working hours or a change to your start or finish time make a difference? If you work shifts, can you change your shift pattern or your days off?

- What about changing your break or lunch times? Or, you could ask for more frequent, shorter breaks throughout the working day.

- Can adjustments be made to your physical workspace? Would somewhere quieter or a bit livelier help you adjust to work?

- Is there a quiet room in the workplace that you can access to get some privacy, or a 'safe space' where you can get some time out?

- Is there an opportunity for you to work from home? It's important that this doesn't have the effect of isolating you, so think about how you could do this while still staying connected with the organization and your colleagues.

- Can your employer agree to give you time off for appointments relating to your mental health, such as counselling sessions?

- Can some of your tasks be reallocated in the short term, or could changes be made to your duties? Alternatively, could you be redeployed to a different role?

- Is there additional training, support or mentoring that you could receive? This might include training to help you build your resilience and coping skills.

- Can your manager offer you greater supervision or support? And can they offer you more feedback on your work, taking regular opportunities to discuss, review and reflect on your positive achievements?

Regardless of the adjustments that are put in place for you, it is important to revisit and reflect on the impact they're having. This will give you and your employer the opportunity to tweak and change them as required, and ensure that the support you've put in place is effective.

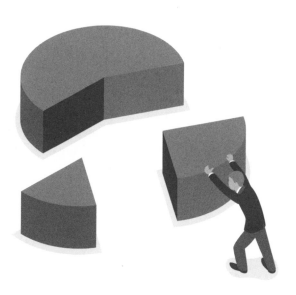

# MANAGING AN ONGOING MENTAL ILLNESS IN THE WORKPLACE

Having an ongoing mental health condition doesn't mean that you aren't capable of continuing to work effectively and perform at a high level within your organization.

And, just as importantly, there is no reason why you should be treated any differently than another employee within your organization because you have a mental health condition. If you are, you're being discriminated against. It is not lawful for your employer to make assumptions about your capabilities based on your mental health issues.

Most people who have ongoing mental health issues continue to work successfully in their jobs, and not every case demands specific support from an employer. Where support is necessary, it is important that your employer is flexible and that you're in agreement on what is required.

Your company's established management procedures for reviewing performance, work planning and employees' individual needs should take into account your needs if you have an ongoing mental health issue. So, work at establishing a positive relationship with your employer, one that leverages an open, two-way channel of communication. That can make all the difference, allowing you to discuss how you're doing and what they can do to help.

As part of your ongoing care and recovery, you will have been encouraged to develop coping strategies. These can be small things that can prevent longer-term absence or a deterioration in your mental health. One coping strategy might be for you to be able to identify the signs of a possible relapse, and take steps to avoid it. Such countermeasures might include prioritizing time to relax or adjust your work-life balance, as well as increasing the amount of exercise you get and cutting down on alcohol consumption.

You could also talk with your employer about drafting an 'advance directive' or 'wellbeing action plan' that outlines how you'd like to be treated in the workplace in the event that your mental health does decline. This document might include information on the symptoms that management and co-workers should look out for, who can be contacted in the event of an issue and the type of support that would be helpful for you.

# ACCESSING EXPERTS WITHIN YOUR ORGANIZATION

If you want help, there are likely to be qualified experts within your organization who can assist you, offering information or advice on your mental health and wellbeing.

## THE HUMAN RESOURCES TEAM

The Human Resources (HR) team within your organization has a pivotal role to play when it comes to identifying, supporting, protecting and nurturing mental health in the workplace.

Whether it is creating a mental health policy for the organization, designing and delivering training to employees and managers or ensuring compliance with legislation relating to mental health, wellbeing, disability and discrimination, HR is central to how mental health is discussed and 'normalized' within a workplace.

The HR team is also a strong internal resource to help managers support employees with mental health struggles, either by ensuring that they're following established procedures and policies to support and manage employees, or acting as a sounding board for a manager's questions about these matters.

HR can direct an employee to the specialist support services that are in place to assist with mental health issues, as well as answer any questions they might have.

# YOUR MANAGER

We've talked a lot about managers' involvement in all this, and it's important not to overlook or underestimate their role in supporting and protecting your mental health and wellbeing in the workplace.

Management provides an important channel for you to talk about mental health concerns and ask for advice on coping with stress and pressure in the workplace. Your manager will also monitor your work environment, performance and changes you've jointly agreed upon to support your mental health.

Managers are a conduit between you and the organization, looking out for signs of mental health issues and balancing the needs and priorities of all parties to ensure that you ultimately have the support, information and advice you need to keep mentally healthy in the workplace.

# EMPLOYEE ASSISTANCE PROGRAMMES

As mentioned, an EAP is a workplace programme designed to assist with productivity and attendance issues, supporting employees by identifying and resolving personal concerns and issues that may be affecting job performance. These might include health, marital, family, financial, alcohol, drug, legal, emotional, stress or other personal issues.

An EAP acts as a gateway to a range of services and support, including:

- Counselling and other short-term psychological services
- Money advice and debt management
- Childcare and eldercare information services
- Legal information and guidance
- Information on emotional, work-life and workplace issues
- Management referrals and support
- Management support on workplace interventions.

An employee's use of an EAP service is voluntary and the vast majority of people who take advantage of them do so through self-referrals. As such, one of the most essential functions of an EAP is its ability to provide confidential support services, on demand, when they're needed and free of charge to employees.

EAPs accept referrals from other groups within an organization, including trade union representatives, HR professionals and managers. The specific way in which each of these referrals is managed will depend on the individual company and will always take into account the employer's HR policies, as well as data protection regulations.

The EAP delivers consultation and training for managers and supervisors within an organization, giving them the opportunity to discuss workplace issues and challenges they might be facing, and providing support and guidance on how to manage these situations in a constructive way.

Information on how to contact your organization's EAP will be available from your HR team or on your company's intranet.

# OCCUPATIONAL HEALTH

Occupational Health services within an organization can support mental health and wellbeing in a number of ways. For instance, they are involved in:

- Conducting health assessments to ensure that employees are fit to perform duties in the workplace, whether by statutory requirement or simply as a good employment practice. This is an important aspect of health, safety and wellbeing management.

- Monitoring for signs of work-related ill health, enabling organizations to comply with current legislation and preventing mental and physical problems from developing. This helps ensure that procedures are in place to effectively manage any health risks.

- Offering management advice and support on employee performance and attendance matters, helping managers determine why an employee may have an issue with attendance and recommending the best support options, especially if mental health problems are a factor.

- Providing management with information on health trends, underlying issues and areas for improvement when it comes to managing workplace health and wellbeing.

Occupational Health professionals can also help with rehabilitation and provide advice, treatment and support that will help you to get back to work or get back to your expected performance levels as quickly as possible.

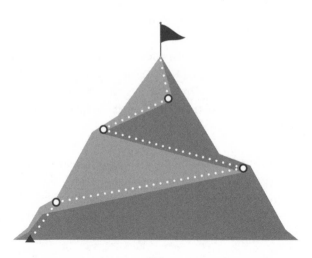

# WHAT TO KNOW ABOUT MENTAL HEALTH AND RECRUITMENT WHEN JOB-HUNTING

Discussing mental health with your manager can be a challenge when you're already working for an employer, but when you're looking for a new job, the question of whether to disclose these issues to a prospective employer can be a tough one to answer.

On the one hand, the more honest you are with a prospective employer, the better they can support you in managing your mental health. However, for many people who do struggle with their mental health, it's not necessary to ask for or receive any specific support for their condition.

As a result, and due to the stigma that's still attached to mental health problems, sharing details of your struggles with a prospective employer is something that needs to be carefully considered.

Clearly, there isn't a right answer here and you might want to find out more about the organization and its employees before opening up about mental health issues you might have had in the past.

Reflecting on some of the following questions might help you decide on the best course of action:

- How would disclosing your mental health issues impact your mental health? Would it take some pressure off, or do you think it would create additional stress for you?

- Do you regularly take any medication that could have side effects that can influence your ability to do the job or work with others?

- Do you have enough information on what the job you're applying for entails?

- What do you know about the culture of the company or the team that you might be working with? Have you had an opportunity to meet them as part of the recruitment process?

- Do you honestly think your mental health might impact your ability to do the job you're applying for?

- Would knowing about your mental health issues help management offer the support you need and make any necessary accommodations?

You can also consider whether there is a positive aspect to your mental health issue that might benefit your job application. For example, can you provide examples of where your condition has given you better insight into supporting others or empathizing with how they might be feeling? Or, would it make you a better manager when it comes to supporting others who might be experiencing mental health issues?

You should also note that if you do have mental health problems and decide not to tell your manager, you cannot expect them to work with you on managing your mental health.

Of course, if you do disclose a mental health condition to a prospective employer, employers in many countries cannot discriminate against current or potential employees on the basis of their disability. This legislation extends to the recruitment and retention, promotion and transfer, training and development, as well as dismissal of employees.

Here, 'disability' is defined as a physical or mental impairment that has a substantial and long-term adverse effect on a person's ability to carry out normal, day-to-day activities. Your mental health issue could be considered a mental impairment, and therefore your employer must also consider whether there is any type of support or accommodations they could make to enable you to do the job.

# +PART 4
# WHAT TO
# DO NEXT?

# MANAGING MENTAL HEALTH AND WELLBEING

Ultimately it only takes one small change to start to make a positive difference in your mental health, but this change has to be driven and managed by you. Here are some suggestions on what you can do to better manage your own mental health and wellbeing going forward.

- **Identify and build support networks:** Think about the support networks that are available to you, find out how to take advantage of them and face up to the fact that it is ok to ask for help. Sometimes just being with people and enjoying their company is a great boost.

- **Be transparent:** Accept that it is also ok to let others know when things are difficult. Everyone feels vulnerable at some point, so avoid getting trapped in a persona of someone who always copes.

- **Don't put all your eggs in one basket:** This includes not putting all your focus on work and neglecting your personal life and priorities.

- **Think about how you manage your time:** Take regular breaks for rest and relaxation when you're at work. Just because you may be working away from home or within a small team, don't be tempted to work 24-hours every day. This will only result in stress and burnout.

- **Establish realistic expectations for yourself:** It is important not to be a perfectionist, so give yourself a break and accept that mistakes will happen. How you learn and recover from these will shape your experience and your future.

- **Take care of yourself:** Do something positive to look after yourself, such as eating well, exercising, getting enough sleep and watching your alcohol intake. Make self-care an essential part of your daily routine.

- **Get enough rest:** Are you going home at a reasonable time? Are you taking all your holiday allocation? Are you looking at your work emails at home, just before going to bed or during the middle of the night when you can't sleep?

Work-life balance is important and you need to ensure that you're creating quality rest time outside of work.

- **Deal with problems effectively:** Changing your perception of a problem may help you find a solution. For example, think about what you can change about a situation or the way others perceive it, or talk through strategies for handling difficult problems with someone you trust.

- **Communicate assertively:** Try and find a balance between not bottling up feelings and not over-reacting. Try to communicate clearly, in a way that's respectful of yourself and others, and be comfortable saying 'no' when you need to.

- **Remain calm under pressure:** Think about what you can realistically do to change a situation. If there is nothing you can do about it, step back, remain calm and avoid making a rushed response. Sometimes something as simple as 'counting to ten' gives you a greater sense of perspective and helps avoid a knee-jerk reaction.

- **Get some perspective:** You can render smaller irritations irrelevant if you compare them with larger and more complex issues and situations. As the saying goes, 'Don't sweat the small stuff'. It's good to remember this from time to time.

- **Create positive experiences:** Do something to incorporate positive experiences into your daily life and routine. It's a good exercise to think what your ideal day would include, and then think about what you could do to make this dream a reality. What do you need to change in order to make this happen?

# HELP AND SUPPORT

Your doctor is usually the first point of contact if you wish to access mental health services. In addition to assessing an individual's circumstances and offering appropriate treatment, medication or advice, the doctor can refer you to a psychological therapy or specialist mental health service for further advice or treatment. There may also be organizations that offer counselling, coaching or stress management courses. Getting to know what is available, and then plucking up the courage to make contact, is probably the hardest – but also the most important – step in moving forward.

It only takes one small change to start to make a positive difference in your mental health.

# THE MENTAL HEALTH TOP TEN: KEY POINTS TO REMEMBER

Mental health is something we all 'have' and experience – it is very personal to us and changes throughout our lives as circumstances change. One in four adults and one in ten children experience a mental health issue during their lifetime, and many more of us know and care for people who do.

It is helpful to think of mental health as being on a spectrum or a scale, and appreciate that 'we all have some days that are better than others'. Where we are on this scale, such as having a difficult day does not have to define us.

An important part of keeping physically well and mentally healthy is to take care of yourself, and there are plenty of things you can do. We've touched on each of these earlier, but here are our top ten tips to achieve better mental health.

## 1. Get plenty of sleep

Sleep is really important for our physical and mental health. Sleep helps regulate the chemicals in our brain that transmit information. These chemicals play a key role in managing our moods and emotions. If we don't get enough sleep, we can start to feel depressed or anxious.

Organizations such as The Sleep Foundation provide tips on how to overcome problems with sleeping [https://sleepfoundation.org/sleep-tools-tips/healthy-sleep-tips].

## 2. Eat well

Eating well is not just important for our bodies, but also for our minds. Certain mineral deficiencies, such as iron and vitamin B12 deficiencies, can give us a low mood. As such, aim to eat a balanced, healthy diet and drink plenty of water.

If you find that you're a particularly stressed or anxious person, try limiting or cutting out caffeine, as it can make you feel jittery and anxious. And remember that caffeine is not just in coffee – tea, energy drinks, supplements, soft drinks and chocolate can all have caffeine in them, and often in higher quantities than you might think!

**3. Avoid alcohol, smoking and drugs**
Drinking and smoking can impact your mental health.

When you've had a few drinks you can feel more depressed and anxious the next day, and it can be harder to concentrate. Excessive drinking for prolonged periods can also leave you with a thiamine deficiency. Thiamine (vitamin B1) is important for brain function and a deficiency can lead to severe memory problems, coordination problems, confusion and eye problems.

Withdrawal – the set of symptoms one experiences when decreasing or discontinuing the use of medications or recreational drugs – is known to be especially challenging to mental wellbeing. If you smoke, between cigarettes your body and brain go into withdrawal, which makes you irritable and anxious. Other drugs will leave you in withdrawal and can often cause very low moods and anxiety. More severe effects of drug use include paranoia and delusions. Some research suggests that drug use is related to the development of mental disorders like schizophrenia.

## 4. Get plenty of sunlight (but not too much!)

Sunlight is a great source of vitamin D, which is important for our bodies and our brains. It helps our brains release chemicals that improve our mood, like endorphins and serotonin. Try to go out in the sun when you can, but make sure you keep your skin and eyes safe. Thirty minutes to two hours a day of sunlight is ideal. During the winter, some people become depressed because they aren't getting enough sunlight – this is known as Seasonal Affective Disorder (SAD). Some people find that using a special light-therapy lamp helps to alleviate these symptoms.

### 5. Manage stress

Stress is often unavoidable, but knowing what triggers your stress and how to cope with it is key to maintaining good mental health. Try to manage your responsibilities and worries by making a list or a schedule of when you can resolve each issue.

If you break down your worries and stresses and make note of them, you'll often realize that they are manageable. Try to avoid burying your head in the sand and tackle problems face on. If you find you're having trouble sleeping, or are waking up thinking about all of the things that are stressing you out, write them down and reassure yourself that you can deal with them in the morning. Keeping a pen and paper beside your bed so you can note down your worries is a good way of managing your sleep time stress.

### 6. Do something you enjoy

Try to make time for doing the fun things you enjoy. If you like going for a walk with the dog, spending time with friends, painting or watching a certain TV show, try to set aside time for those activities and enjoy yourself. If we don't spend any time doing the things we enjoy, we can become irritable and unhappy.

**7. Find time for physical activity and exercise**
Activity and exercise are essential for maintaining good mental health.

Being active not only gives you a sense of achievement, but it boosts the chemicals in your brain that help put you in a good mood. Exercising can help eliminate low mood, anxiety, stress and feeling tired and disengaged.

You do not need to run a marathon or spend hours in the gym; a short walk or some other gentle activity often does the trick.

Taking exercise with other people, and sharing your worries and concerns along the way, is often a good way of improving how you are feeling.

**8. Connect with others and be sociable**
Make an effort to maintain good relationships and talk to people whenever you get the chance. Having friends is important not just for your self-esteem, but also for providing support when you're not feeling too great. Research has found that talking to others for just ten minutes can actually improve memory and test scores.

### 9. Do things for others

Helping others is not just good for the people you're helping, it's good for you too.

Helping someone can boost your self-esteem and make you feel good about your place in the world. Feeling as though you are part of a community is in fact a really important part of your mental health. You could try volunteering for a local charity, or just being neighbourly.

### 10. Ask for help – and do not be embarrassed to do so

One of the most important ways to keep yourself mentally healthy is to recognize when you're not feeling good, and know when to ask for help. There is no shame in asking someone for support if you're feeling low or stressed. Everyone goes through patches where they do not feel as good as they should.

You can try speaking to your friends or family, or if you think your mental health is in decline you can speak to your GP or, if you have one, an EAP provider.

Those with mental health problems have been stigmatized for centuries, and too many people – especially men – have received no help at all.

Many people have not received positive mental health services or have had to wait many months before getting these services. This is really not acceptable, especially given the significant impact that poor mental health can have on our communities.

But the future is looking brighter; in recent years the picture has started to change for the better. Public attitudes towards mental health are improving, and there is a growing commitment among communities, workplaces, schools and across society to change the way we think about it.

To help change thinking on this important public health issue, please share these top tips – and ideally this book – with those who might need it. You can and should be part of the movement to destigmatize mental health problems, raise awareness and give parity to mental health alongside physical health.

# OUR BENEFICIARIES

This book has been jointly funded and sponsored by Royal Mail Group and Optima Health. All proceeds from the sale of this book are being donated to the following two charities:

## THE ROWLAND HILL FUND

The Rowland Hill Fund was established in 1882 as a memorial to Sir Rowland Hill, the great postal reformer and founder of the modern British postal service, who retired as Secretary of the Post Office in 1864.

Over the years, the fund has helped thousands of individuals. In its early days, before the existence of the 'Welfare State' or the introduction of occupational pensions, organizations such as the fund were often the only place people could turn when in financial distress. However, although welfare provision is now an accepted part of society, there is still financial distress, and the Rowland Hill Fund is still a vibrant organization.

The fund deals with a wide range of cases and the diverse nature of the help it is able to provide reflects an ongoing need for the financial support it gives.

Due to the ever-increasing cost of living, the fund encounters many situations that produce genuine difficulty for individuals and their families. It is uniquely positioned to help Royal Mail, Post Office Limited and any of the associated companies' people who are in financial distress.

For more information, visit **www.rowlandhillfund.org**

# ACTION FOR CHILDREN

Action for Children was founded in England over 147 years ago.

The organization helps disadvantaged children across the UK, from before they are born until they are into their 20s.

The organization helps them through fostering or adoption and by intervening early to stop neglect and abuse. It helps make life better for children with disabilities and works to influence policy and advocate for change.

Action for Children's 7,000 staff and volunteers operate more than 600 services, improving the lives of 370,000 children, teenagers, parents and caregivers every year. The group succeeds by doing what's right, doing what's needed, and doing what works for children.

For more information, visit **www.actionforchildren.org.uk**

# ABOUT THE AUTHORS

## DR SHAUN DAVIS

Shaun is Global Director of Safety, Health, Wellbeing and Sustainability for Royal Mail Group.

He is also a Chartered Fellow of the Institution of Occupational Safety and Health, a Fellow of the International Institute of Risk and Safety Management, a Chartered Fellow of the Chartered Institute of Personnel and Development, and a Member of the Institute of Directors. He was also appointed Honorary Assistant Professor at the University of Nottingham's School of Medicine in February 2018.

Shaun holds five master's degrees: an MA in Leadership & Culture Change, an MBA, an MA in Marketing & Innovation, an MSc in Workplace Health & Wellbeing and an MA in Strategic Human Resource Management. He is currently studying towards a Master of Laws (LLM).

Research for his doctorate in Coaching and Mentoring explored the relationship between coaching, wellbeing and organizational culture, examining how coaching influences employee wellbeing and productivity.

Shaun is currently a trustee of three charities: The Rowland Hill Fund (Trustee and Deputy Chair), The Men's Health Forum and The Society of Occupational Medicine. He is also a member of the Business in the Community (BITC) Workwell Leadership Team and a Member of the National Forum on Health and Wellbeing in the Workplace. In addition, he acts as Vice Chair and Director of Strategy for the pan-European mental health campaign 'Target Depression in the Workplace' [www.targetdepression.com].

Follow Shaun on Twitter at **@DrShaunDavis**

# ANDREW KINDER

Andrew is a Chartered Counselling & Chartered Occupational Psychologist and Registered Coach with the British Psychological Society, is the Past Chair of the British Association for Counselling and Psychotherapy's Workplace Division [www.bacpworkplace.org.uk] and was awarded a Fellowship from BACP for his contributions to workplace counselling. He is an Associate Fellow of the British Psychological Society, and a Registered Practitioner Psychologist with the Health and Care Professions Council. Andrew has two diplomas in counselling, an MSc in Occupational Psychology and is a Senior Accredited BACP Counsellor.

He has published two academic books with co-editors Professor Sir Cary Cooper and Rick Hughes – *Employee Wellbeing Support: A Workplace Resource* and *International Handbook of Workplace Trauma Support.* His latest works, again with the same co-editors, are the self-help books *The Crisis Book* and *The Wellbeing Workout.*

Andrew is an experienced practitioner with 25 years' experience. He works as a counsellor, mediator and coach. He has been published widely and is particularly interested in the management of work-related mental health and trauma within organizations. He is currently the Professional Head of Mental Health Services at Optima Health. He has been instrumental in the introduction of early intervention programmes in a number of large organizations, relating to employee engagement, remote working, wellbeing strategies, psychological trauma and employee wellbeing.

He is Past Chair of the Employee Assistance Professionals Association [www.eapa.org.uk] and in early 2018 the group awarded him an Emeritus Membership for his work in the employee assistance industry. Andrew is also a Trustee with the British Association for Counselling and Psychotherapy.

For more information on Optima Health,
visit **www.optimahealth.co.uk**

For more information on Andrew,
visit **www.andrewkinder.co.uk**

# ABOUT THE
# BOOK'S SPONSORS

## ROYAL MAIL GROUP

Royal Mail is the UK's pre-eminent delivery company. We deliver more letters and parcels, to more addresses in the UK, than all of our competitors combined.

We are proud to deliver a 'one-price-goes-anywhere' service on a range of letters and parcels to around 30 million addresses, across the UK, six-days-a-week, in our role as the UK's sole designated Universal Service Provider. Royal Mail has deep cultural roots and these have helped to shape the history of the UK and the way the world communicates for over 500 years.

We also make a very significant contribution to the wider UK economy, through UK Parcels, International & Letters (UKPIL), our impact and value-add, including through employment and procurement, is significant.

General Logistics Systems (GLS), our pan-European parcels business, operates one of the largest ground-based deferred parcel delivery networks in Europe.

For more information, visit **www.royalmailgroup.com**

# OPTIMA HEALTH

Optima Health is a leading UK occupational health and wellbeing company. We help organizations and their people perform at their best by managing their health.

We have an extensive employee team of over 320 occupational health practitioners in the UK: consultant physicians, occupational health nurses, occupational therapists, physiotherapists, counsellors, psychologists, technicians, registered nurses and physiologists.

We work across a range of sectors, both public and private. Within the private sector we specialize in the energy and utilities, construction, manufacturing, rail, transport and financial sectors. We also provide services to blue light organizations and are one of the largest providers to the NHS, and to central and local government.

We know that one size doesn't fit all. So, our preference is to work with organizations to understand their requirements. This way we can create integrated, compelling and multidisciplinary solutions where, together, we focus on outcomes, measuring value and return on investment for the organization.

For more information, visit **www.optimahealth.co.uk**

25TH

**LID**
ANNIVERSARY

Sharing knowledge since 1993

- 1993  Madrid
- 2008  Mexico DF and Monterrey
- 2010  London
- 2011  New York and Buenos Aires
- 2012  Bogotá
- 2014  Shanghai